Islamic Activism and U.S. Foreign Policy

Islamic Activism
and U.S. Foreign Policy

Scott W. Hibbard and David Little

UNITED STATES INSTITUTE OF PEACE PRESS
Washington, D.C.

United States Institute of Peace
1550 M Street NW
Washington, DC 20005

First published 1997

Printed in the United States of America

The paper used in this publication meets the minimum requirements of American National Standard for Information Sciences—Permanence of Paper for Printed Library Materials, ANSI Z39.48-1984.

Library of Congress Cataloging-in-Publication Data
Hibbard, Scott W., 1962–
    Islamic activism and U.S. foreign policy / Scott W. Hibbard and David Little.
      p. cm. — (Perspectives series ; 5)
    ISBN 1-878379-71-2 (pbk.)
    1. Islamic countries—Foreign relations—United States. 2. United States—Foreign relations—Islamic countries. 3. Islam and politics. 4. Islam—20th century.
    I. Little, David, 1933– . II. Title. III. Series.
DS35.74.H53 1997
327.73017'671—dc21   97-21908
                                                                     CIP

CONTENTS

Summary   VII

Foreword   How Should Policymakers Respond to the
Challenge of Islamic Activism?
by William B. Quandt   XIII

Preface   XXV

Introduction   3

1. Iran   29

2. Algeria   37

3. Jordan and the Palestinians   49

4. Pakistan and South Asia   65

5. Turkey *by Patricia Carley*   79

6. Indonesia   95

Conclusion   107

Notes   113

Participants   135

SUMMARY

Political violence in the Middle East and elsewhere has come to symbolize for many people the threat of "Islamic activism." This perspective frequently assumes that the phenomenon—also referred to as "Islamic fundamentalism" or "political Islam"—represents a common and coordinated threat to the West. For others, however, Islamic activists are seen as neither unified nor necessarily hostile. What, then, is the nature of Islamic activism and what does this mean for U.S. foreign policy?

These issues were the basis for a series of meetings hosted by the United States Institute of Peace between 1994 and 1996. The dominant theme of the Institute series was the dilemma faced by U.S. policymakers who must deal with the political violence of extremists in countries where political, economic, and social reforms are very much needed. Implementing such reforms, however, may inadvertently strengthen groups who have no more commitment to human rights or democratic norms than the regimes they seek to replace.

In the course of the Institute meetings, two different interpretations of Islamic activism emerged, and, with them, two different policy approaches. The first approach distinguished between moderate activists (those who advocate social reform in a manner consistent with democratic values) and extremists (those who condone the use of violence to achieve antidemocratic ends). Since, according to this approach, most Islamic activists are first and foremost social reformers, the best policy is one of inclusion and accommodation. Tolerating, or co-opting, the moderate opposition isolates the extremists and minimizes the threat of violence and radicalism. The second approach, however, rejects the significance of distinguishing between moderates and extremists. Regardless of the methods they may employ, all activists have fundamentally the same goals: the establishment of an authoritarian theocratic state. Consequently, a policy of exclusion and repression is not only warranted but also essential.[1]

U.S. policy has sought to address the basic concerns of both these viewpoints. The Clinton administration, like its predecessor, has articulated its opposition to political violence and its commitment to addressing the economic and social ills that generate support for extremism. According to administration officials, the problem is extremism, not Islam.

Implementing this approach, however, is not easy. Policymakers must balance the often competing goals of long-term democratic development, on the one hand, and short-term regional interests (such as stability and access to energy resources), on the other. One way of achieving this balance is to promote political and economic policies that gradually cultivate "civil society" in at-risk countries. Accordingly, policymakers would avoid equating democracy with its formal trappings, such as elections, and instead work toward encouraging an independent sector of society devoted to tolerance, voluntary participation, and nonviolent reform. The objective is to create stability and accountable government by developing the conditions that support democracy, rather than trying to impose it abruptly and artificially.

IRAN

Iran was the first case study examined. Participants generally agreed that the revolution is now dead insofar as public support for the Islamic agenda has waned. The Iranian regime, it was argued, retains only a narrow base of domestic support, and many observers feel it will ultimately collapse of its own weight. For the foreseeable future, however, oil revenues and lenient European trade policies seem to ensure the regime's survival and continued ability to fund militant groups around the world. Several participants noted, also, that the policy of containment and isolation pursued by the United States may have shored up the regime's legitimacy by casting it as an abused victim.[2] Since neither indulgence nor isolation alone is likely to change the regime's behavior, it was argued that an alternative approach might be effective—one that opens Iran to outside influences and more directly links financial support and trade to Iran's international actions.

ALGERIA

The situation in Algeria epitomizes the dilemmas facing U.S. policymakers. In that country, competing and frequently violent militant Islamic groups seek to reshape Algerian society. Although such groups justify their actions as a fight against the forces of corruption and sacrilege, they have demonstrated little commitment to democratic values and the tolerance of dissenting views. However, the ruling regime has been demonstrably undemocratic and has for several years pursued a policy of "eradication" in dealing with its Islamic opposition. As one participant noted, "In Algeria, there are no good guys."[3]

The future of Algeria remains uncertain. One policy alternative offered in the Institute roundtable was to support a serious dialogue among all political parties in Algeria, similar to the one initiated by the Italian lay Catholic group Sant'Egidio in pursuit of national reconciliation. Unfortunately, subsequent events, including the November 1995 presidential elections, marginalized the Sant'Egidio process, and national reconciliation, as well as economic and political reform, is still needed. To this end, a more proactive U.S. policy could help. It is argued that the United States should be "more engaged with the [Algerian] regime and encourage it down a road it says it wants to pursue. . . . namely, a return to normal life, reform [of] the economy, a rebuilding [of] political institutions, parliamentary elections, and so forth."[4] Whether the current government of President Lamiane Zeroual can achieve such goals will determine whether its approach to the challenge of Islamic activism is successful in the long run.

JORDAN AND THE PALESTINIANS

In the third meeting in the series, the Institute working group examined the Islamic movements in Jordan, the West Bank, and Gaza. Islamic activism in this area illustrates both the diversity of Islamic organizations and the competing tendencies within specific groups over both means and ends. In the West Bank and Gaza, the political exclusion of the Palestinians appears to have contributed to the militancy of Hamas and Islamic Jihad, while in Jordan a policy of political inclusiveness has produced a degree of accommodation between Islamic activists (particularly the Muslim Brotherhood) and the government. These organizations, however, are not uniform. Although Islamic activists generally

agree, theoretically, on ultimate ends, factions within organizations have struggled over how best to achieve their goals.

The implications for policy remain mixed. Despite repressive measures, violence carried out by members of Hamas has hindered the Middle East peace
process and increased pressure on both Israel and the Palestinian Authority to
respond with greater force. In Jordan, the effort to co-opt Islamic activists has
also not been entirely successful. Despite a policy of limited inclusion, activists
retain an assertive mood based on their opposition to the peace process with
Israel. There is also concern that continuing confrontation by Islamic activists
may lead Jordan—like Israel and the Palestinian Authority—to respond more
forcefully to the challenge of Islamic activism. As a result, the tension between
political liberalization and opposition to a negotiated settlement with Israel
may restrict movement toward democracy and peace within the region.
"[Consequently], contrary to many optimistic forecasts, . . . the end of the Arab-
Israeli conflict will likely usher in a new era of authoritarianism."[5]

PAKISTAN AND SOUTH ASIA

The Pakistan case also illustrates the diversity of Islamic activism. The Jama'at-
i-Islami (the Party of Islam), a prominent Islamic organization influential
throughout the Islamic world, has historically worked within the political
process, rather than standing for violent resistance and revolution. The inclusion of the Jama'at in the political system, it is argued, has mitigated its ideological demands and shaped its largely accommodationist methods. Although
never able to secure power in its own right, it has been extremely influential
through grassroots activism and its ability to define political debate.

Although the Jama'at has been influential, its predominance in Pakistan is
diminishing. Assertive "sectarian" parties have emerged recently that represent
a special challenge for U.S. policy. These new groups are less focused on doc-
trinal purity, and are influenced more by the "Kalashnikov culture" of the region. Their strength derives from access to sophisticated weaponry left over
from the Afghan war, funding from abroad, and the absence of government control. These groups are, in part, unintended consequences of the Cold War strategy to arm the *mujahidin* during the 1980s. As former ambassador Robert
Oakley commented during the Institute discussion, once the Afghan war was
over, the network established to support the *mujahidin* began "looking for a
cause, [and] the militants . . . for something to do."

TURKEY

Turkey demonstrates yet another variation of how government policy and Islamic activism interact. In Turkey, Islamic activism has not been a significant force politically, though it has long been represented in the electoral system, most recently by the Islamic party Refah (Welfare). The relative weakness of the Islamic activists is due in part to Turkey's unique history and to a strong sense of Turkish identity. Of greater significance, however, is the explicitly secular and democratic political system in Turkey. This relatively open political system has mitigated the development of Islamic extremism in Turkey, and the existence of mediating institutions, including a vibrant civil society, keeps a check on extreme swings in Turkish political life.

Despite its historical weakness, the current Islamic party, Refah, won a plurality of votes in the December 1995 parliamentary elections, and subsequently established a coalition government. It is not yet clear what this development will mean for the future. Early indications, however, appear to signal little radical change. Despite opposition among many of Refah's core supporters, the Refah prime minister, Necmettin Erbakan, adopted many of the previous government's policies in order to gain the support necessary to form a ruling coalition. Furthermore, it is argued that Refah's electoral success does not represent the ideological challenge many people fear; on the contrary, many of the people who currently support Refah do so for economic rather than ideological reasons. Many observers—and even Refah leaders—acknowledge that Refah benefited significantly from those voting in protest against the two dominant political parties that have alternately ruled Turkey over the past ten years.

INDONESIA

The last case study examined was Indonesia, the world's largest Islamic country. This country has not been plagued in recent years with the kind of religious extremism, violence, and intolerance that are present in other areas. On the contrary, Indonesia's "New Order" regime, which has ruled Indonesia since the 1960s, has based its tenure on the twin pillars of national unity and religious pluralism, even if it had to rely upon military rule to enforce these policies.

Although there seems to be no significant "threat" of Islamic extremism in the conventional sense, the centrality of Islam in Indonesian politics has increased over the past decade. This is due, first, to a stronger sense of Islamic identity among Indonesians, and, second, to the ruling regime's use of Islam as a means of supporting its rule. While the overall trend is clear, the implications remain less so. Many people are concerned that this "greening" (or Islamization) of Indonesian politics may fuel intercommunal tensions and threaten the country's tradition of religious tolerance.

However, this environment, coupled with Indonesia's phenomenal economic development, has also produced a flowering of Islamic modernist thought. "Concurrent with the growth of the Islamic middle class has been a self-conscious attempt on the part of a small group of Islamic intellectuals [the so-called neomodernists] to develop a more open, tolerant and pluralistic approach to the relationship between state and Islamic society."[6] The resonance of this interpretation of Islam gives some analysts reason to believe that Indonesia may be the "cradle for [the] growth of tolerant Islam."[7]

FOREWORD

How Should Policymakers Respond to the Challenge of Islamic Activism?

William B. Quandt

Ever since the Cold War came to a sudden end at the beginning of this decade, Americans have been debating foreign policy priorities. One of the frequent candidates for a new "-ism" to rally against is "Islamism." The publication of this volume, *Islamic Activism and U.S. Foreign Policy*, is an occasion to ask whether Islam, in any of its variants, is really a threat to American interests in a way that might be seen as analogous to communism in the 1950s and 1960s, and if so what can the United States do to deal with such a challenge. If not, we still need to ask how we should conduct our relations with Muslim states and political movements.

The debate over political Islam spans a spectrum from fairly sophisticated arguments about the increasing role of values and culture as dividing lines in international affairs—the "Clash of Civilizations" thesis—to simple journalistic visions of a "green peril." For most Americans, it seems, Islam is a poorly understood religion, associated with disparate menacing images such as those of Iran's Ayatollah Khomeini, Libya's Muammar Qaddhafi, and even Nation of Islam leader Louis Farrakhan. The memory of Americans held hostage in Iran and Lebanon reinforces the popular belief that there are deep incompatibilities between Muslims and the United States.

Despite these indications that Islam is somehow seen as a threat by many Americans, it is striking to note that the United States has quite good relations with most Muslim countries—Egypt, Indonesia, Morocco, to mention just a few—and American officials go to considerable lengths to stress that Islam is a religion deserving of respect, not a source of problems for American foreign policy. Presidents Bush and Clinton have both publicly stated that they see no basis for hostility between the United States and Islamic countries. On the domestic front, millions of American Muslims go about their daily lives quite normally. If Islam is not the problem, then what, if anything, is?

The debate surrounding Islamic activism and American foreign policy has a certain similarity to the debate over communism in the middle third of this century. In the 1930s, many saw communism as an understandable response to the economic crisis of the depression and to the rise of fascism in Europe. Then, as now with Islamic militancy, it was easy for intellectuals to become apologists for an ideological system that seemed idealistic, egalitarian, and anchored in a strong sense of community in contrast to the rampant individualism of capitalism. The horrors of the Stalin era were still not widely known, or were treated as aberrations.

In the 1940s, many Americans swallowed whatever distaste they felt for communism and treated Stalin as a worthy ally in the fight against fascism. Something similar happened in the 1980s when Americans cheered on the Islamic warriors in Afghanistan who were battling the occupying Soviet army. But once the common cause was ended, in both cases perceptions quickly changed. Stalin became a bloody dictator in popular American perceptions—no more "Uncle Joe"—and the noble *mujahidin* warriors were seen as misogynist fanatics reveling in a "Kalashnikov culture."

Perhaps the most revealing comparison of American attitudes toward communism and Islamic militancy can be found in the period of the 1950s and today. During the 1950s, a real debate took place over the nature of the communist threat. Was it primarily ideological, or was the danger fundamentally related to Soviet power? Could the threat be dealt with by deterrence and containment, or did it require more active measures of opposition? Were the main communist powers working together in the international arena, or could one drive wedges between them? Were socialists and radical nationalists little more than fronts for communists, or were they potentially valuable allies in the struggle against communism? Could one weaken the appeal of communism, especially in Third World settings, by addressing underlying social and economic issues? Would time and circumstance work to moderate communism and turn it into a harmless political movement akin to social democracy?

At various times, different sides of these debates had strong followings, but by the end of the 1950s there seemed to be something of a consensus. Not all communist regimes were the same. The United States could have good relations with Yugoslavia's Tito, "peaceful coexistence" with Russia, and no relations at all with China, while actively trying to undermine communist regimes on the periphery of the big power blocs. Nationalism in the Third World was not automatically seen as equivalent to communism, and European Social Democrats were recognized as allies in the competition with the Soviet bloc. Soviet power, more than the ideas of Marx, Engels, Lenin, and Mao, was seen as the major threat, and containment, based on the assumption that in due course communism would change from within, provided a bipartisan foundation for American foreign policy for much of the remainder of the Cold War. The great exception to this consensus in the 1960s, of course, was Vietnam, where the debate was resolved only after the death of fifty thousand American soldiers and a rethinking of the place of China in the global scheme of things.

As the current volume demonstrates, many of the arguments concerning political Islam have a familiar ring to them. There is still no consensus on key issues. Is there an Islamic "essence" that is fundamentally hostile to Western values and to ideas of democracy and pluralism? Or is Islam, like other great religions, subject to a variety of interpretations at different times and places? Are moderates and extremists among Islamic activists simply two wings of the same movement, both of which seek to impose Islamic law and pursue a militant struggle with all non-Muslims? Or are moderates and extremists deeply different in their goals and tactics, and if so, can those difference be exploited by those who fear Islamic radicalism? Can Islamic political parties function in democratic settings, or will they use any opening to seize power, then suspend democratic procedures, as Hitler did in the 1930s—the "one person, one vote, one time" phenomenon?

Needless to say, these issues are debated in a highly politicized context. It would be a mistake to believe that so-called experts or informed sources are free of political agendas of their own. For example, many of the regimes in power in the Middle East are intent upon promoting a view of Islamic radicals as beyond the pale, sponsored by Iran or Sudan, and irrevocably committed to violence. Much of the information available to policymakers comes from such sources. Many Israelis, apprehensive about the views of Islamists toward Zionism and the peace process, support this interpretation and find themselves championing Arab leaders and regimes whom they used to abhor. These voices are also listened to in Washington. From time to time one even gets a hint that Saddam Hussein will try to work his way back to respectability in the West by presenting himself as an anti-Islamist who supports the Arab-Israeli peace process.

Just as critics of Islamist activists have their own political agendas, so often do their supporters. Many in the academic community are offended by simplistic caricatures of Muslims, and tend to bend over backward to make distinctions between legitimate grievances of Islamic movements and the violent extremists who also claim to speak for Islam. And they see a double standard when human rights violations by incumbent regimes are tolerated, while the excesses of Islamist movements are pointed to as evidence that they are little more than terrorists.

To say the least, there is little meeting of minds among observers and analysts about the nature of Islamic activism. And yet policymakers cannot wait until a consensus emerges. They need sensible guidelines and some notion of the range of reasonable interpretation, and they cannot be expected to become experts on Islam and its political manifestations overnight. Most frequently, they will take their cues from highly self-interested and biased sources. But if dealing with Islam and its political offspring is really likely to be a major issue in the years ahead, we must try to understand the nature of the diverse challenges to American interests that are mounted in the name of Islam, and we must have some reasoned discussion about policy responses.

A careful reader of this volume will come across a number of themes that deserve serious attention. Each can help policymakers form judgments about concrete issues.

▶ The cases reviewed here, which include Iran, Algeria, Jordan and the Palestinians, South Asia, Turkey, and Indonesia, reveal a remarkable diversity of Islamic movements. There is no equivalent of the Comintern—a central clearinghouse for Muslim activists. Each country seems to have Islamic movements that reflect distinctive political experiences of that country. Some regimes that consider themselves Islamic are quite open to close relations with the West—Saudi Arabia is a case in point—and others show a measure of support for democracy and pluralism, such as Turkey, Pakistan, and Malaysia.

▶ Despite the diversity that one finds among Islamist movements, there are also common themes and cross-border relations that cannot be ignored. For example, Islamic movements are almost all hostile to Israel and critical of some aspects of Western power and values. In opposition, Islamic movements tend to appeal to the disenfranchised, the "oppressed," the marginal, promising greater social justice, an end to corruption, and that "Islam is the solution." They tend to be short on programs and specifics, and long on

idealism and rhetoric. In power, Islamist parties often find it difficult to retain popular support. They have no magic solutions to the problems of society; they have no unique Islamic economic model; they end up relying on
force and abusing human rights; and the claim of ruling in the name of Islam
is not enough to maintain legitimacy indefinitely.

▶ Where Islamist movements have long traditions and have been tolerated by
regimes—Turkey, Pakistan, Jordan, Indonesia—they have generally refrained
from violence and from total challenges to the political system. This suggests
that it may be possible, in some circumstances, to domesticate and moderate Islamic political movements by giving them voice. But where Islamic
movements have emerged more recently in sharp reaction to the perceived
failures of the nationalist model, as in Algeria and Gaza and the West Bank,
it may be more difficult for regimes to co-opt or domesticate Islamic militants. Their initial goal is to take over the system entirely, not to reform it.
Their moderate wings can easily be outflanked by militants willing to use violence. In other words, the likely success of a policy of co-optation depends
very much on the nature of the regime itself—whether or not it has reser-
voirs of legitimacy to draw on—and the nature of the opposition. The anal-
ogy with communist parties may again be instructive. French and Italian
communists participated in elections after World War II and eventually mod-
erated their programs and recast themselves as social democrats; in many
Third World countries, communist parties remained illegal and militant, beyond co-optation and unreformable. Regimes there were too weak to risk
allowing communists to participate in political life, and the parties themselves were too narrowly based to compete for power through legal means.

▶ In a number of countries, very violent groups have emerged that claim to be
Islamic. In some cases, there is a direct link to the Afghan war, which produced a hardened, disciplined cadre of fighters from a variety of countries.
Today in Algeria, Pakistan, and Egypt, these veterans of the Afghan war are
among the most radical and intolerant of all Islamic activists. Incumbent
regimes often argue that there is a seamless web linking these radicals and
more "moderate" Islamists. This is probably not usually the case, but it is often true that the militants can outbid the moderates, driving them to silence
or making them appear to be in complicity with unpopular regimes. For example, in Algeria the Armed Islamic Group (GIA), while small in numbers,
has contributed to undermining the more popular Islamic Salvation Front
(FIS). It is no exaggeration to say that some of these extremist groups are

little more than armed gangs, often with strongly fascist overtones. The head of the Algerian GIA (a veteran of the Afghan war) was quoted in January 1997 as saying, "Except for those who are with me, all the others are apostates and merit death." It is hard to imagine what basis there might be for accommodation with such a movement. Attempts by Western powers to engage with such movements in the hope of moderating them will be futile and will further serve to undermine the credibility of other political movements, including Islamists, that are willing to eschew violence and play by democratic rules.

▶ As a political phenomenon, Islamic activism must be seen in context. It is a movement that grew out of the failure of the nationalist project in many parts of the Muslim world; it often identified itself with popular and populist causes; it received a boost from the Iranian revolution and the Soviet invasion of Afghanistan; and it has probably begun to lose its broad appeal as the record of Islamic regimes in power is seen as wanting. This does not mean that Islamic movements pose no challenge to the existing political order, but predictions that Egypt, Algeria, or Saudi Arabia are about to fall to radical Islamist challenges seem far from the mark. At least one serious scholar has already written of the "failure of political Islam." In Iran, some who initially supported the role of the clergy in politics are now calling for more distance between the state and religion, a development that could be important for Iran's eventual return to less militant politics. Outside of Iran, the revolutionary Iranian model is rarely mentioned as one to be emulated. The other Islamic republic, Sudan, is something of a pariah in both the Middle East and Africa and continues to struggle with a long-running civil war.

▶ As powerful as political Islam may seem as an opposition movement, it has never managed to win a majority in a free election. Even in Algeria in 1990–91, most Algerians either abstained or voted for non-Islamist parties. Of the total Algerian electorate, only one-third voted for Islamist parties in 1990 in local elections, and only one-quarter the following year in parliamentary elections. In Turkey, which had an Islamist prime minister between 1996 and 1997, the Refah party came in first in the 1996 elections, but with about 20 percent of the vote. In the Palestinian elections in January 1996, Islamists generally did not run, but public opinion polls indicated that their support was considerably less than 20 percent. In Jordan and Kuwait, Islamist candidates have recently lost to conservative candidates with strong tribal support. In short, democracy does not always work to the advantage of Islamists. Much depends on the other parties and how they manage to form coalitions.

▶ Much time and energy has been spent on the theoretical debate over the compatibility of Islam and democracy. This study suggests that, in certain circumstances, the two can be compatible, but it is still difficult to find many convincing examples. Turkey, Pakistan, and Malaysia, along with Jordan and Yemen, are cases that suggest that Islamic political movements can engage in competitive politics along with other political parties. But in each case there are other powerful actors to check the ambitions of the Islamists. The Iranian case suggests that when an Islamist movement seizes power and eliminates its major competitors through force, it will not be willing to risk its newfound power through genuinely free elections.

▶ Since experience to date does not provide a conclusive answer about Islam and democracy, we are tempted to look at Islamic political theory for answers. As with any religiously based political movement, there is bound to be a question about the ultimate source of authority. Does legitimate authority flow from God (as interpreted by someone claiming to know His will) or is sovereignty rooted in the people? In theory, Islam leaves no room for doubt. God is sovereign. But in practice, Muslims have experimented with a wide array of political institutions and have not recognized that rulers are above the law. If there is something distinctive about Islam and its political theory, it is that institutions have been devalued in favor of the "just leader" who can interpret God's law for the community of believers (as Muhammad did for his followers), and today's Islamic regimes are measured against an ideal set by the first Islamic state—that of Muhammad in the seventh century. Thus, there is a tendency toward idealism and the search for the just leader on the part of Islamic activists that does not always fit easily with the give and take of democratic politics. This is not to say that Islam and democracy are incompatible. Most religions do not fit easily with practical politics. But it does suggest that there is little in Islamic political theory that is a natural ally of democracy, other than, perhaps, the emphasis on the rule of law.

▶ No Muslim country, and no Islamic movement, poses a threat to the United States in any way comparable to that posed by the Soviet Union in the 1950s and 1960s. Most are economically weak, militarily underdeveloped, and quite vulnerable to American and Western counterpressures. This does not mean that acts of terror cannot be mounted by radical Islamists, but such threats are quite different from the type of challenge that the Soviets presented to Western Europe, or Saddam Hussein posed to the smaller Gulf states.

▶ Muslim states have not been noteworthy for their levels of cooperation. In fact, there are more fault lines among Muslim states than between them and any other political grouping. Algerians are suspicious of Moroccans; Syrians and Iraqis are at loggerheads; Egypt and Sudan are often quarreling; Iran, Afghanistan, and Pakistan are all at odds. There is little reason to believe that Muslim unity will soon arrive. Thus, whatever the nature of the challenge from specific Islamist movements or regimes, the United States is unlikely ever to face a unified Islamic threat. When the United States has found itself at odds with Islamic regimes, as with Iran, it has found many allies such as Saudi Arabia on its side. Raison d'état still trumps ideology in most of the Islamic world.

American policymakers will be well advised to reflect on some of the themes of this study. The world of Islam is not unified or monochrome. Islam as a faith is not the same as the political activism that seeks to legitimize itself by invoking the symbols of Islam. Most Muslims, and most regimes in Muslim countries, pose no particular problems for American interests. We are still very far from the much-hyped "Clash of Civilizations." There is nothing inevitable about such a clash, as numerous American political leaders have already made clear in their public comments.

A realistic appreciation of the nature of the Islamist challenge, however, does not necessarily lead to a posture of passivity. There are, after all, steps that can be taken by the United States that might reduce the likelihood of serious disputes between Americans and Islamists. Policies generally need to be tailored very much to the specifics of individual countries—such as American policy toward Turkey's relations with Europe—but there are also some broad themes that need attention.

For better or worse, the United States is now deeply involved in the negotiations between Israel and its Arab neighbors. If these stalemate or fail, many Islamists will blame the United States, and many ordinary Muslims will agree with that judgment. Regimes that have cooperated with the United States in the peace process (the Jordanian, Egyptian, and Palestinian regimes, for instance) will come under pressure from more radical voices, some speaking with an

Islamist accent. As the negotiations approach the final-status issues in coming years, it will be increasingly difficult for the United States to avoid taking positions on substantive issues. For example, will the United States recognize the Israeli claim to all of Jerusalem and move the U.S. embassy there? Will it continue to oppose the creation of a Palestinian state? Will it support the idea that Israeli settlements can remain in the midst of the West Bank? If so, one should expect a backlash of some magnitude on the part of many Muslims. By contrast, an American position on these issues that is judged to be fair by moderate Muslims will help to strengthen those in the Islamic world who argue for cooperation with the West.

In addition to promoting a just and secure peace between Israel and its neighbors, the United States should try to ensure that at least one of the Muslim countries with which it has close ties will emerge as something of a model of economic and political development. So far, no country in the Islamic world stands out as a model of economic and political reform in the way that South Korea, Taiwan, or any number of Latin American countries do. That is to say, we cannot point to a case of successful American-supported economic and political development that has resulted in sustained economic growth, social progress, and democracy. The big recipients of American aid in the Muslim world, such as Turkey and Egypt, could play important roles in their regions if they were to be seen as successful in their development. While the United States cannot make development happen, it can continue to encourage those policies that seem to have the best chance of bringing about economic progress and political liberalization. Of all the Muslim countries, Egypt and Turkey are probably the two where success would redound most to America's advantage, while also protecting tangible geostrategic interests in the region. Smaller, but also important cases might be Jordan and the territories controlled by the Palestinian Authority. Aid, trade, and investment need to be used intelligently to promote development, and high-level political contacts will be required to try to develop a shared sense of purpose between the United States and existing regimes.

How should the United States deal with comparatively friendly authoritarian regimes that confront Islamist challenges, such as Algeria or Tunisia? Some would argue that a policy of strong support is the only viable option. Others make just the opposite case, citing Iran as an example of the need to open contacts with those who oppose unpopular regimes before they come to power. There is something unsatisfactory in both of these positions.

Those who urge full backing for incumbent anti-Islamist regimes seem to believe that the Iranian revolution could have been avoided if only Jimmy Carter had not criticized the Shah for his human rights record. There is scant evidence for this conclusion. No regime has fallen to Islamist opposition because it has been too mindful of human rights. On the contrary, the regimes that are the most flagrant abusers of human rights seem most vulnerable to Islamist challenges.

Those on the other end of the policy spectrum seem to believe that U.S. relations with postrevolutionary Tehran could have been fine if only we had cut our ties to the Shah at an earlier date. This view ignores the usual dynamics of revolution and the near inevitability that a new Islamic regime would have found itself at loggerheads with the United States even if we had maintained a dialogue with Khomeini before the revolution.

Where, then, should policymakers come down on this issue of dealing with unpopular incumbent regimes facing Islamist challenges? First, the United States should recognize that it usually has only marginal influence at best. Second, a status quo power such as the United States cannot be expected to try to unseat existing regimes, even if they are unpopular. Third, even friendly regimes should not be exempt from criticism on matters ranging from economic policy to human rights. But the most effective means of raising such issues is likely to be in private. This requires an ongoing dialogue even with regimes that we may not much care for. Fourth, some contacts with Islamist opposition groups are probably useful, but should be handled carefully and with an awareness of the political signals being sent. Fifth, if and when Islamists come to power, the United States will generally want to try to develop normal working relations with them, counting on mutual interests to overcome ideological antagonisms. Sixth, Europeans often have similar views on these matters and we should try, where possible, to coordinate policies to maximize the chance of having some impact.

Although most acts of international terrorism regularly occur in non-Islamic settings, there is still a popular perception, and some reality, that links terror attacks to some Islamist movements. What can the United States do about this type of threat? The answer has nothing specifically to do with policy toward Islam, but rather is part of the more general problem of fighting militant armed groups that are intent on using terror to advance their causes. The only sensible course seems to be a combination of heightened intelligence work; cooperation with other countries in tracking and neutralizing the activities of these groups; and prudent steps to make it difficult for terrorists to attack sensitive targets. But this issue belongs in a discussion of terrorism more generally, since there is nothing particular that sets Islamist terrorists apart from others. If the issue, however, is state sponsorship of terror, then we should focus on how to deal with the offending state.

Finally, there is the question of Iran and how the United States should manage its relationship with this self-styled beacon of Islamic radicalism. It is tempting to think that Iran today is a bit like China in the 1950s in terms of American foreign policy. The idea of an American opening to Iran, just as the idea of recognizing "Red China" then, is practically taboo in political circles. And yet the regime in Tehran seems to be entrenched, it is dealing quite normally with most of our allies, and sanctions have done little to curb its revolutionary ardor. At some point, almost inevitably, the United States and Iran will need to deal with one another. The question is on what level and on what terms. There is no easy answer, but we might begin by recognizing the failure of the containment policy to date; and we might open the public discussion on alternatives, rather than simply referring to Iran as a "rogue," or "gangster," or "backlash" state. If at some point the United States and Iran come to be on speaking terms, this will send a signal to Islamist movements elsewhere that the United States is not uniformly hostile to Muslim interests. This is not so much a matter of searching for elusive Iranian moderates, but of dealing with Iran on matters where our interests are engaged, much as we do with other difficult regimes. In time, there no doubt will be moderates in power in Iran, but more because of Iranian political dynamics than anything the United States can do. Still, it does little good to try to keep Iran isolated, and the legislation that seeks to punish firms investing in Iran's oil industry is likely to be counterproductive.

In addition to some of the steps mentioned above, there are also a number of small steps that can help to build a foundation for better relations between the United States and Muslim countries in the future. First, there is still a great deal of interest among Muslims in studying in the United States and in learning English. While cultural and educational exchanges do not always work miracles, they can present a strong and attractive feature of our society and can help to create points of contact that may be useful in the future. The cost of these programs is minor compared to the benefits, but Congress needs to hear the case over and over again for why they serve American interests.

Second, the United States cannot expect to have a sophisticated policy toward Muslim countries without the intellectual resources to know what is actually happening in those countries. This means that scholars who study the history, politics, and languages of these regions need support, without political strings attached. Funding through the Pentagon and CIA is still too compromising for most academics to tolerate. Other sources need to be provided to ensure that American students are able to study the world of Islam, learn its languages, travel among its people, and eventually improve their understanding of the Islamic world. Certainly, the United States benefited during the Cold War from having a group of scholars and students who were knowledgeable about Russian and Chinese societies and spoke their languages. Such programs are not a panacea, but they are a lot better than the ignorance that will otherwise be the basis for policy.

Note what is missing in this discussion of policy options. Nowhere does it seem as if the United States will be called upon to undertake a massive military buildup to meet the Islamic threat. Nowhere do we hear calls for big increases in economic aid. Mostly what is called for is sensible diplomacy and an investment in understanding a region of the world that still seems mysterious, and perhaps ominous, to many Americans. This should not be too big a challenge to meet, even in the post–Cold War era.

PREFACE

In 1994, the United States Institute of Peace initiated a series of roundtable discussions to examine the phenomenon of Islamic activism and its implications for U.S. foreign policy. The goal of the project was to better understand not only a variety of manifestations of Islamic activism but also how different government policies—ranging from repression to inclusion—influence the development of activist organizations. By approaching these issues in a comparative manner, the project sought to identify patterns among regions and countries and the effectiveness of different policy responses, both by governments within Islamic countries and by the United States.

The end result of this project is the following report. The report summarizes the proceedings of the various meetings hosted by the Institute between June 1994 and February 1996. Although the report is by no means exhaustive, it has sought to portray these discussions accurately and to identify the themes of greatest import for policymakers and students of U.S. policy. The report presents a survey of diverse cases that can provide a useful overview to a very complex issue. The cases were chosen because they exemplify the diversity of the Islamic world, and not just of the Middle East.[1]

In the course of these discussions, a working group was assembled to examine the cases of Iran; Algeria; Jordan and the Palestinians; Pakistan and South Asia; Turkey; and Indonesia. The participants included government officials, academics, journalists, and foreign policy specialists. There was little consensus in the discussions, reflecting the wide divergence of opinion among both the participants and the Washington policy community regarding both the nature of Islamic activism and how policymakers should respond to it. There were, however, several recurring themes and topics that dominated the discussions.

Two key issues identified in the seminars are (1) why certain activists advocate and use violence to achieve their goals while others do not, and (2) whether efforts by some governments to "co-opt" such movements do, in fact, work. Although the answers to these questions are complex, the case studies provided valuable insights.

Concerning the first issue, the resort to violence appears to be rooted in both the marginalization (and radicalization) of certain populations and the tactical effectiveness of using violence to achieve political ends. Quite simply, persons with little stake in a given political system are more prone to militancy. Efforts to isolate and eradicate militants, though somewhat successful in quelling violence, do not address the long-term, social, economic, and political problems that generate support for such extreme tactics. Also of concern are the long-term ramifications of repressive policies. Both of these issues are discussed in this report.

Regarding the second issue, the case studies illustrate that efforts to co-opt Islamic activist movements have met with mixed results. Although in countries such as Pakistan, Turkey, and Indonesia, the participation of certain groups in the political process has had a moderating effect on their behavior, such efforts have also had the side effect of "Islamizing" the political debate, often with deleterious consequences for minority groups. The case studies thus highlight the complexity of Islamic activism and provide insight into the role of religion in the political life of a number of different Islamic countries.

A report such as this is, of course, time-sensitive. Even so, efforts have been made to update the text to reflect key developments through 1996 and early 1997. Furthermore, the depiction in this volume of the basic issues and perspectives of the debate over Islamic activism will not soon be outdated. Care has been taken to accurately portray not only the differences of opinion and outlook among the participants in the Institute discussions but also the views of other experts whose opinions were solicited or whose writings were consulted. Having laid out the competing interpretations and proposals, the report leaves the task of evaluating the different approaches to the reader.

This report builds on earlier work of the United States Institute of Peace concerning both Islamic activism and the role of religion in politics. An early effort by the Institute in this area included a conference held in May 1992 that culminated in the publication of *Islam and Democracy: Religion, Politics, and Power in the Middle East* by Timothy Sisk. The Institute also hosted a symposium in March 1994, in conjunction with Georgetown University's Center for

Muslim-Christian Understanding, entitled "Political Islam in the Middle East: Its Regional and International Implications." Some of the papers and discussion from that conference are referenced in this report. Finally, the Institute's special initiative on Religion, Ethics, and Human Rights has been involved in a multiyear study of religion and ideology, with a particular focus on intolerance and discrimination as sources of international conflict, and, conversely, on the role of religious tolerance as a necessary condition for peace.

The authors would like to thank the many participants in the conference series "Islamic Activism and U.S. Foreign Policy" for their contributions and thoughtful comments, particularly those who prepared papers and those who commented on the various drafts of this manuscript. Special thanks go to William Quandt, Robert Oakley, Adnan Abu-Odeh, Samuel Lewis, Tahseen Bashir, Mona Yacoubian, Maen al-Nsour, Eric Goldstein, Steve Riskin, Robert Satloff, Sara Simon, Abdullahi An-Na'im, Nigel Quinney, and Dan Snodderly. Those who presented and/or commented on papers include Shaul Bakhash, Andrew Whitley, William Zartman, Robin Wright, Glenn Robinson, Martin Kramer, Vali Nasr, Robert Oakley, Sugata Bose, Serif Mardin, Morton Abramowitz, William Liddle, and Don Emmerson.

Islamic Activism and U.S. Foreign Policy

INTRODUCTION

Political violence in the Middle East and elsewhere symbolizes for many people the threat of "Islamic activism."[1] This perspective frequently assumes that the phenomenon—also known as "Islamic fundamentalism," "Islamism," or "political Islam"—represents a common and coordinated threat to the West. Others, however, reject this point of view, and argue that Islamic activists are neither unified nor necessarily hostile. What, then, is the nature of Islamic activism? Why is it perceived to be a threat to U.S. interests? Is there a reliable difference between Islamic extremists and moderates? If so, how should U.S. foreign policy respond to that difference?

These questions were addressed in a series of discussions held at the United States Institute of Peace between June 1994 and February 1996. Although there was no consensus—a fact that reflects a wide divergence of opinion among the participants—there were several recurring themes and topics.

The central topic of the Institute meetings was the dilemma faced by U.S. policymakers who must deal with the political violence of extremists in countries where political, economic, and social reforms are badly needed. Attempts to deal with one set of problems often work against efforts to deal with the other. Government actions to contain extremism are often at odds with the longer-term goals of democratization and market liberalization. Similarly, implementing needed political reforms may inadvertently strengthen, or even bring to power, groups who have no more commitment to human rights or democratic norms than the regimes they seek to replace.

The differing approaches to this basic dilemma, as articulated in the Institute meetings, divided over competing interpretations of Islamic activism and, specifically, whether or not a significant distinction exists between moderate

3

and extremist Islamic activists. The case studies indicate, on the surface at least, that Muslims committed to radical reform are not unified, particularly concerning the issues most important to Western policymakers, such as restraining violence and working out political compromise. Radical Islamic groups appear to vary from time to time and from place to place. What members do in Algeria or Pakistan is not what they do in Jordan or Iran. Some use violence (or condone its use) to achieve political ends, while others—apparently more pragmatic or moderate—choose to operate within existing political systems.

If there is in reality a significant and reliable difference between extremists and moderates among Islamic activists, that difference, together with their respective prospects, is something policymakers need to know about. What is an appropriate response to one group may not be an appropriate response to another.

But is this distinction valid? Again, the Institute working group participants split on whether all Islamic activists are inherently extremist or whether a meaningful distinction can be made between those who advocate a militant approach to change and those who shun violence in favor of religious piety and pragmatic social reform. Policy decisions in specific cases are determined largely by whether or not this distinction between moderates and extremists can be sustained. In the debate, two alternative policy approaches emerged.

One position, ardently represented in the Institute discussions and supported in certain scholarly circles,[2] rejects the significance of distinguishing between moderates and extremists, and rejects the argument that mainstream activists' movements have an underlying yearning for democracy. Whether activists work within the system or oppose it from outside, their ultimate objective, according to this line of argument, is the same—namely, to replace the existing order with an authoritarian Islamic state. This goal is said to reflect their fundamental convictions, which consistently deny pluralism, compromise, and genuine tolerance.[3] "While fundamentalist groups and ideologies differ from each other in many ways, all of them are inherently extremist and all despise our civilization. . . . They might, for tactical reasons, modify or suppress these aspirations but they do not abandon them. By definition, fundamentalists seek a way of life deeply incompatible with our own ideals."[4]

Proponents of this position reject out of hand the notion that accommodation with Islamic activists is possible or that those activists can be counted on as steadfast supporters of democracy. Iran and Sudan are cited as examples of what happens when Islamic activism takes power. According to this view,

Islamic activism is more akin to aggressive nationalism than religious revival, and the leaders "more like Zhirinovsky than Havel."[5] A policy of confrontation and exclusion of all activists is then taken to be the best approach for dealing with this phenomenon.

The opposing position, also well represented in the Institute discussions, affirms the distinction between moderates and extremists. According to this view, so sprawling a phenomenon as Islamic activism covers a wide and shifting complex of ideals, objectives, interests, and members. Some parts of the movement are perceived to be susceptible to accommodation and even co-optation within a pluralist political system, given the appropriate combination of inducements and circumstances. Without such inducements, however, activists are likely to adopt more extreme, and often violent, measures in the name of advancing what they believe to be the cause of Islam.

According to this second account, Islamic activism is dynamic and diversified. It is not so much made up of fixed and stable constituencies, as it is animated by competing moderate and extremist *tendencies* that can be activated with varying degrees of appeal and intensity, depending on conditions.

When the conditions are propitious, a policy aimed at encouraging democratic participation can help consolidate moderation and discourage extremism. A policy of inclusion, it is argued, will provide activists with a stake in the system and motivate them to "play by the rules." Consequently, they will have to subject their programs to electoral tests and, in competing for power, will be compelled to form coalitions and practice compromise.[6] In addition, a policy of inclusion can have a moderating effect by overcoming the sense of marginalization and dispossession that breeds extremism. "By the very fact that they [are] illegal, unrecognized Islamist movements have no motivation to accommodate their opponents and embrace democracy and [they have] ample incentive to take as rejectionist a stance as possible."[7]

Finally, it is argued that "tarring" all Islamic activists with the same brush is self-defeating, and potentially detrimental to American interests.[8] Perceiving all activists as inherently extremist fosters indiscriminate repression and justifies Western support for regimes opposed to Islamic activism, no matter how undemocratic, repressive, or unpopular such regimes may be. Obsession with the "extremist peril," and the urgency of subduing it, can divert attention from the economic and political infirmities that appear to give rise to extremism, and from the need for responding with imaginative and progressive policies, instead of mere force and repression. "It is partly the case that . . . Islamists look like they have the best chances . . . where the regimes are doing the worst jobs. It is not that Islamism is an unstoppable wave."9

In its broad outlines, current U.S. policy has sought to address the basic concerns from both of these perspectives. The Clinton administration has emphasized its ardent opposition to political violence and extremism—religious or secular—and also the need to address underlying causes of extremism. On May 17, 1994, National Security Adviser Anthony Lake described the perspective of the United States as follows:

> In the Middle East as throughout the world, there is indeed a fundamental divide. But the fault line runs not between "civilizations" or religions. No, it runs instead between oppression and responsive government, between isolation and openness, between moderation and extremism. . . . Our foe is oppression and extremism, whether in religious or secular guise. We draw the line against those who seek to advance their agenda through terror, intolerance, or coercion . . . . There should be no doubt [that] Islamic extremism poses a threat to our nation's interests. . . . [It flows] from common sources: disillusionment, a failure to secure basic needs, dashed hopes for political participation and social justice. Widespread disenchantment breeds an extremism of hatred and violence—an extremism by no means unique to the Middle East or the Muslim World.[10]

The question, remains, however, whether the distinction between moderates and extremists holds up, and whether it can be relied upon as a basis for making policy. The problem is important not only for deciding whether moderate activists can become steadfast allies of peaceful pluralism, but also whether it is possible, under some conditions, to make moderates out of extremists, and whether the cause of moderation can be advanced without losing the capacity to contain extremist violence and disorder.

Another important dimension of policymaking, mentioned but not resolved in Lake's statement, is the broader question of "our nation's interests." The problem of balancing long-term goals with short-term strategic and economic interests is nowhere more perplexing than in the Islamic world. On the one hand, reforms pursued too quickly can be profoundly destabilizing, and may play into the hands of nondemocratic opposition groups. On the other hand, efforts to contain extremism may be accompanied by the excessive use of force that at once intensifies extremist hostility and discourages even moderate reform. Paradoxically, such action may have the long-term effect of undermining the very conditions of political and economic security that suppressing extremism was supposed to ensure.

THE ORIGINS AND CHARACTER OF ISLAMIC ACTIVISM

Background

The link between religious revival and political reform is a common theme in Islamic history. During periods of decline, reformers have often sought to reawaken religious devotion as a means of redeeming the political community. Loss of faith and subversion of the ideals of Islam were taken to be the cause of social ills, and the prescribed remedy was a "return to Islam,"[11] including renewed commitment to "the Qur'an, the life of the Prophet, and the early Islamic community."[12] The possibility of using force to attain these ends—while always controversial—was very much a part of the deliberations of the reformers.

The origins of contemporary Islamic activism are to be found in the Muslim reaction to European colonial rule in the late nineteenth and early twentieth centuries. After several centuries of military and political preeminence, Islamic centers of civilization came under the control of the emerging European powers. This was a defining experience for many countries—particularly in North Africa and the Middle East—and constituted a profound spiritual as well as political crisis. The dominance of Western ideas, technology, and institutions forced many Muslims to reevaluate not only their political situation but also the deeper issues of religion and society.

Islamic reaction to Western domination took three forms. First, some Muslims, like the influential Egyptian theologian Muhammed Rashid Rida, advocated withdrawal into a defensive and conservative posture, rehearsing and taking comfort in the traditions and past accomplishments of Islam.

> The main concern of most orthodox theologians and the great theological seminaries . . . was to safeguard and preserve the normative and institutional structures of tradition from the increasingly aggressive onslaught of Western ideas and institutions. In order to achieve this objective, the ulama [religious leadership] established a network of [traditional Islamic educational institutions] . . . in which they sought to preserve the purity of tradition. . . . [These] became the center for the reassertion of Sunni orthodoxy and a focus of conservative opposition to modern Western thought and institutions.[13]

A second group of Muslims, also affected by Western education, were more receptive to the Western way of life. These were the "modernists," who undertook to demonstrate the compatibility between Islam and the premises, methods, and ideals of Western civilization. Arab thinkers like Khalid Muhammed Khalid and Muslim reformers from the Indian subcontinent, such as Sayyid

Ahmad Kahn, Muhammad Iqbal, and Sayyid Amir Ali, all proposed what might be called a policy of "constructive engagement" with the West. Ali, for example,

> sought to demolish the Western and Christian notions of their intellectual and religious superiority over Islam and defended his faith with the help of the intellectual apparatus he had acquired through English education. He challenged Western critics of Islam on such questions as the role and status of women in Islam, the institution of slavery, the treatment of non-Muslims under Islam, and the conflict between reason and revelation.[14]

The third and at present the most publicized form of response is Islamic activism. The Muslim Brothers of Egypt (founded in 1928) and the Jama'at-i-Islami in South Asia (founded in 1941) are the two groups that have most influenced and shaped this category. They mobilized Muslims around a message of "aggressive self-assertion,"[15] and established what would become a dominant pattern of activist thinking. In the process, they both absorbed and rejected certain elements from the conservative and modernist positions.

On the one hand, these groups honor the traditions and past glories of Islam, and what are considered to be the authentic fundamentals of the faith. They also tend to be familiar with Western ways and thinking, and a good number of their leaders are Western-trained, especially in technical fields such as engineering. They have little hesitancy in making use of Western techniques in communications, economics, and technological development.

On the other hand, both conservatives and modernists are believed to have fallen short of the Islamic ideal and are in part responsible for the deteriorating condition of Islam. By escaping into tradition, and perpetuating their sterile conventions, conservatives fail to exploit Islam's potential for shaping and influencing the modern world. According to the activists, modernists go too far in the opposite direction and simply capitulate to the West. Unfaithful to their own tradition, they are seen as disfiguring the clear message of Islam and recasting it in a Western image.

The two variations of modernism that had a particularly strong effect on Islamic activists—particularly in the Arab world—were Arab nationalism and Arab socialism. Arab nationalism sprang to life after World War I, partly in response to the collapse of the Ottoman Empire and to the ascendancy of the nation-state system. To strive for national self-determination was to be accepted as a respectable member of the international community. In keeping with Western ideals, the nationalism of this period was generally "secularist, believing in a bond which could embrace people of different schools or faiths, and a policy based upon the interests of state and society." It was also "constitutionalist, holding that the will of the nation should be expressed by elected governments responsible to elected assemblies."[16]

It was not long before support for such Western ideals waned. Appeals for self-determination went unrequited, and nations like Egypt, Syria, and the Maghreb countries either continued under foreign rule or were newly subjected to it. In the face of what was regarded as blatant hypocrisy, Arab nationalism turned to virulent anticolonialism, spurning many Western liberal ideals, such as constitutional democracy and individual liberty, and raising doubts about the applicability to Islam of the idea of a secular public sphere. In some cases, the Arab independence movement even fell under the influence of European fascism, something that only strengthened the antipathy to Western liberalism.[17]

Arab socialism came into fashion after World War II, and was in many ways an extension of Arab nationalism. It strongly espoused certain modernist themes—economic and social improvement based on the development of new industry and technology, the expansion of education and medical services, and a concerted effort to reduce the role of religion in public life. These themes all bore the mark of Western influence.

At the same time, Arab socialism was resolutely anticolonial and expressed itself in the independence movements of the 1950s in Egypt, Syria, the Maghreb, and elsewhere. Moreover, the "socialist" emphasis on collectivization, state ownership, and central planning, partly influenced by Marxism and Maoism, represented an intention to disown the liberal, free market ideas of the West and to shape a distinctive and independent way of life based on the overarching unity of Arab peoples born of a common language and culture.[18] The success of this movement owed much to the leadership of Gamal Abdul Nasser of Egypt, as well as to a common opposition to the existence of Israel.

Although coming to power in Iraq, Egypt, Algeria, and Syria and significantly influencing the politics of the Arab and Islamic worlds, the socialist parties ultimately failed to maintain their popular support. This failure was due largely to their inability to resolve existing economic problems, the Arab defeat in the 1967 war with Israel, and the death of the charismatic Nasser in 1970. Their demise, however, was also attributed by some people to the socialists' weak commitment and, in some cases, outright hostility toward Islam,[19] something directly associated with the corrosive influence of Western "secularism."

Both of these twentieth-century movements were modernist in the sense that they borrowed heavily from the West in the process of reforming the social and political ideals of Muslim societies. At the same time, they were also a reaction against the West and the continued colonial influence of pro-Western Arab regimes. They therefore served to discredit Western ideas and institutions throughout the Muslim world and to generate a spirit of revolutionary fervor.

Islamic Activism

Islamic activism succeeded Arab nationalism and socialism as the principal revolutionary threat to established regimes in a large number of Arab and other Muslim countries.[20] Activists have tapped into the same anti-Western sentiment associated with Arab nationalism, and have used a deep sense of humiliation and frustration among Muslim populations to advance their cause. Their rhetoric is laced with political and economic critiques of the status quo, and they argue forcefully for a return to Islam as the authentic, indigenous alternative to Western models of social organization and development. In short, Islamic activism has become a "potent ideology of popular dissent."[21]

> Islam provide[s] an effective language of opposition: to Western power and influence, and those who could be accused of being subservient to them; to governments regarded as corrupt and ineffective, the instruments of private interests, or devoid of morality; and to a society which seemed to have lost its unity with its moral principles and direction.[22]

The overthrow of the Shah of Iran in 1979—seen by Muslims as a vindication of Islam against the corrupting influence of the West—was a watershed for Islamic activists. It demonstrated the vitality of Islamic political ideology as an independent force, and inspired like-minded activists throughout the Muslim world. The successes in Afghanistan against the Soviet forces further strengthened the idea of Islam as a viable political ideology. Consequently, Islamic activists came to understand the political utility of religion and the effectiveness of using the mosque as a center of protest in countries where opposition was otherwise banned.

Although Islamic activists differ over how best to achieve their goals, they do seek common ends. Above all, activists seek to transform society in accordance with their interpretation of Islamic principles.[23] They attribute the social ills that plague so many Muslim countries to the irreligious or secular nature of their governments and leaders. Since the absence of religion (or religious values) is perceived to be the problem, the solution offered is a return to Islam as the organizing principle of society. This proposed alternative includes, among other things, establishing an Islamic state based on *shari'a* (Islamic law) and drawing religion directly into politics. According to this way of thinking, Islam is "a dynamic and activist political ideology which must acquire state power in order to implement its social, economic, and political agenda. . . . Unlike the conservative[s] . . . and the modernists, [Islamic activism is] primarily [a] political rather than [a] religio-intellectual movement."[24]

The ability of Islamic activists to generate support is attributable to a number of factors.[25] First, the centrality of religion in the daily life of many Muslim countries allows activists and others to use popular religious and cultural sentiments to their own ends. Islam, like other religions, is an important element in shaping individual and collective identity. Consequently, professions of faith are an important source of political legitimacy. Even Egypt's Nasser relied upon appeals to Islam to support his more secular vision of society; "the realities of Egyptian and Arab society caused him to increasingly use or manipulate religion to legitimate his state socialism and broaden his popular support."[26] Whether the appeal to Islam is the result of a genuine desire for social justice or a cynical manipulation of religion for political gain, it remains a potent tool for mobilizing popular support.[27]

A second source of support is the widespread revulsion toward official corruption and the inequities of wealth and opportunity within many Islamic societies. This has been coupled with the proactive efforts by many activist groups to ameliorate the plight of the poor. Movements throughout the Islamic world have identified themselves with the dispossessed, the so-called *mustadhafin*. In Egypt, Gaza, and the West Bank, Islamic activists have gained significant support through their charitable activities. They provide health care, education, and other social services that are not provided by local authorities. "During recent earthquakes in Cairo, it was the [Islamic activists] who put up tents and provided direct assistance to thousands suddenly made homeless, . . . [not the government] which many regard as distant, insensitive, and corrupt."[28]

The concern with economic justice finds resonance in many Muslim societies. While "you cannot explain Islamic movements simply by enumerating economic and political dislocations,"[29] poor economic performance, poverty, and illiteracy are serious challenges for existing governments. Population growth throughout the Islamic world continues to outpace economic development, resulting in high unemployment and a widespread decline in per capita incomes.[30] Urbanization, which is particularly rapid in the Middle East, has

strained aging infrastructures, disrupted traditional ways of life, and stirred social discontent. In many countries, the urgent need for economic reform is
stifled by bureaucratic inertia, corruption, the extreme concentration of wealth,
and the continued dominance of public monopolies. "The economic gap between the 'haves' and the 'have-nots' of the Arab world remains wide."[31]

The preponderance of authoritarian regimes dating from the end of the colonial era has also contributed to the rise of Islamic activism. Widespread repression and the absence of elections have undermined the legitimacy of many
regimes, and strengthened support for virtually any alternative to the status
quo. Since formal opposition is banned in many countries, dissent has been
forced outside the political system and has frequently found expression through
religious organizations. The situation in Iran prior to the 1979 revolution is a
good example of this phenomenon. While political opposition to the Shah could
be contained, the mosques could not be shut down. Similarly, many Islamic
movements, such as the Islamic Salvation Front (FIS) in Algeria, have linked their
religious message with a demand for democratization and greater political participation.

While there has been some political and economic reform in Muslim countries, most notably in Jordan, experts are divided as to how effective such attempts have been. Some analysts argue that many efforts at political
liberalization have continued to exclude large portions of society. They have
been "designed not to inaugurate [an open or democratic system], but to solidify and broaden the base of the elite in power."[32] Other commentators, however, contend that sincere efforts have been made to address these issues, even
if the results are not readily apparent. "While much more can be done, it is im-
proper to dismiss what has been achieved."[33]

Theocratic Tendencies: How Representative?

A central criticism of Islamic activism is the assertion that its underlying ideology is incompatible with constitutional democracy. Many activist thinkers argue that the concept of *tawhid* (the unity of God) contradicts the Western
distinction between secular and sacred realms, and cannot be reconciled with
the separation of church and state.[34] At issue is the inclination to fuse civil status and religious identity, and thereby run the risk of excluding or discriminat-
ing against minority populations and their beliefs. Such an outcome contradicts
basic standards of democracy and tolerance, particularly when the dominant
beliefs are translated into law and discrimination is institutionalized.

The situation in Sudan exemplifies the problem. In June 1989, a military coup brought to power a government closely allied with the National Islamic Front (NIF), an outgrowth of the Sudanese Muslim Brotherhood. Having suspended the constitution and disbanded the elected parliament, the regime implemented an extensive program of Islamization throughout the country. In keeping with that program, the military government appointed a new National Assembly composed of members sympathetic to the NIF, and replaced a large number of judges who were considered ideologically unsound. NIF supporters have since come to dominate in business, law, government, and academia. According to the U.S. State Department's *Country Reports on Human Rights for 1993*, "the NIF-dominated regime pursued religious, ethnic, and ideological discrimination in almost every aspect of society."[35]

The inspiration for this reconstruction of Sudanese society is rooted in a particular interpretation of the Qur'an, the traditions of the Prophet, and *shari'a*. These Islamic foundations, it is argued, provide the basis for a secure, unified, and successful society, capable of repelling the forces of disintegration and demoralization associated with the influence of Western secularism.[36]

Unfortunately, the Islamic foundation of the NIF-backed government has not provided a basis for peaceful national integration in a country with a significant Christian and animist population. The ideology of Islamic activism, as it has been implemented, appears instead to have mobilized a strong form of nationalism that is deeply antagonistic to the rights of free thought and fundamental belief for its minority populations. While the civil war in Sudan is complex, there is no doubt that the Islamic social vision, as formulated by the NIF, is a central element. According to Francis Deng, "an underlying cause of the war" is "the attempt by the north not only to define the identity [of Sudan] as Arab and Islamic, but [also] to structure and stratify the life and role of citizens along those lines."[37] In the more prosaic words of the U.S. State Department, "fear of the imposition of Shari'a remained a key issue in the rebellion."[38]

It is not clear, however, how dominant this exclusivist interpretation of Islamic thought really is. While all activists theoretically endorse the unification of religion and politics, many have, in practice, supported more pluralistic political systems. This is particularly true in Jordan and Turkey. Similarly, in Pakistan, the Jama'at-i-Islami explicitly endorsed a constitution modeled on British parliamentary democracy as consistent with its teachings. Although it fell far short of what the Islamic activists had sought, the constitution contained enough references to the Qur'an and Sunna to appease the leaders of the Jama'at.

The content of the constitution and the kind of state it aimed to create were strongly tilted in the direction of the modernist preferences. In accepting it [Mawlana] Mawdudi [the Jama'at leader], not only seemed to deny much of what he had previously insisted upon as characteristic of an Islamic state but, indeed, left intact very little that would distinguish him from the liberal constitutionalists he had previously so bitterly criticized for their un-Islamic ways.[39]

In a country such as Indonesia, the critique of an exclusivist, theocratic version of Islam comes not, strictly speaking, from other Islamic activists, but rather from a "neomodernist" group of Muslims. Abdurahman Wahid, the leader of Indonesia's largest Islamic organization and an opponent of the ruling regime, has been critical of what he sees as the "sectarian and exclusivist" tendencies of those who use religion for political purposes. An advocate of a pluralist interpretation of Islam and democratic politics, Wahid is involved in an effort within Indonesia to redevelop Islam from the inside, cultivating a tolerant alternative to the exclusivist ideas increasingly prevalent in the country. This neomodernist interpretation of Islam rejects dogmatism, recognizes that God alone possesses absolute truth, and believes that there is no single form of government that can be considered uniquely "Islamic."[40] Similar to Islamic activists, the neomodernists base their work on classical texts, the Qur'an, and the traditions of the Prophet. This interpretation is a very interesting Islamic alternative to extremism.

The Disputed Role of Violence

A second major source of criticism of Islamic activism concerns the use of violence to gain political power. The ruthlessness and violence of *some* activists have weakened the claim that *any* activists would respect democratic norms or international standards of human rights should they gain political power.

From the very beginning, however, a debate has taken place among Islamic activists about the permissibility of and limitations on the use of violence in promoting Islamic ideals.[41] The Egyptian Muslim Brotherhood—the earliest of the activist organizations—became deeply divided over this issue. When it was established, the organization was distinctively and self-consciously nonviolent. Its founder, Hasan al-Banna, shunned the resort to arms and advocated working within the system. However, more extreme members, while sharing many of the same values and goals, eventually split off over the issue of violence, and thus opened the door to the proliferation of violence-prone activist organizations.

Founded in Egypt in 1928, the Muslim Brotherhood quickly attracted a large following, establishing branches in Jordan, Sudan, Syria, Iraq, and other countries. The Brotherhood advocated the establishment of an Islamic state and argued the need for social reform, particularly in the areas of social services and education. It also emphasized the need to protect Islamic culture from what was perceived to be the corrupting influences of Western and secular ideals. Although they were originally apolitical, the Muslim Brothers evolved into an active political organization, and in 1945 al-Banna himself ran for the Egyptian parliament.

In the 1930s, however, a group of dissenters opposed al-Banna's commitment to nonviolent reform, and broke away to establish their own, more militant faction of the Brotherhood. "A debate [then] commenced . . . which continues in Egypt [today] regarding whether or not it is obligatory to engage in holy war to purify society."[42] The militant wing was strengthened during World War II, and in 1952 it found a common cause with a group of young military officers, including Nasser, who took control of Egypt at that time. In two years, however, the militant wing lost faith in Nasser and allegedly attempted to assassinate him. In retaliation, Nasser outlawed the Muslim Brotherhood, and several of its members were imprisoned and executed, including the well-known Sayyid Qutb.

Nasser's crackdown on the Muslim Brothers emboldened militants in Egypt, giving rise to new radical groups, all committed to violent confrontation with the state. While such groups are distinctive in that they advocate the use of lethal force in seeking activist objectives, even they do not defend the unlimited or unrestricted use of force. From among traditional Islamic warrants for using force, militants typically single out appeals to emergency or "states of exception" as a reason for suspending the ordinary restrictions on armed combat.

One such appeal, *The Neglected Duty*, was printed by Islamic Jihad, the militant group responsible for the assassination of Anwar Sadat in 1981, to justify "holy combat to overthrow the unbelieving state."[43] According to this account, all Muslims are victims of oppression and their territory is illicitly dominated by apostates,[44] or "innovators," who are believed to violate the Qur'an and the record of Mohammed's words and actions. Because by their aggressive acts these apostates imperil the very existence of Islam and all it stands for, their rule has no legitimacy and does not need to be respected.[45]

According to *The Neglected Duty*, those persons legitimately engaged in a jihad of survival against illicit rulers are permitted to employ unconventional tactics, like deception, stealth, and spying, both because of the superior might of the government and because the enemy is in a state of apostasy. At the same time, some standard restrictions covering the use of force apparently apply to those conducting a jihad. They are supposed, for example, to try to avoid harming noncombatants or initiating direct attacks against them, although, like anyone operating under the laws of war, they may not be held responsible for the "indirect killing" of such people if it is warranted by military necessity.[46]

This inclination of militants to disregard the ordinary restrictions on using force when there are exceptional circumstances probably accounts for the fact that the charter of Hamas, the militant Palestinian organization, gives no sustained attention to questions of tactics and their limits. Such groups contend, in effect, that the conditions of necessity in which they find themselves require that traditional moral limits "must be stretched."[47] The same interpretation probably also applies to armed insurgents such as the Armed Islamic Group (GIA) in Algeria, giving them an excuse for their direct attacks on women who work as professionals, attend school, or do not wear veils.

The real problem, however, is not that militants fail in practice to honor consistently the restrictions they espouse. Conventional police and military forces do not always scrupulously observe prescribed limits either. The essential difficulty is that Islamic activists who favor violence are inclined to consider themselves exempt from normal restrictions governing the use of force because they perceive their struggle as sacred and their societies as being in a state of emergency. To describe the enemy as an apostate—an enemy of God—is to have an especially significant reason to disregard or minimize the restrictions ordinarily expected under conditions of armed conflict.[48]

This permissive view toward the use of violence, however, continues to be opposed within the ranks of Islamic activism. Some moderate activists explicitly reject the use of violence as incompatible with their vision of an Islamic society, and, if nothing else, as a tactical mistake.[49] Militants seek to impose change upon a society from the top down; however, others (particularly the quietist da'wah element) see social change as flowing naturally from the religious conversion of individuals within society. In this view, the creation of an Islamic society depends on the reform of individual hearts and minds, and the use of force is counterproductive toward these ends.

> Violence can do nothing more than distort da'wah to the path of Allah (SWT). Da'wah seeks to penetrate the innermost recesses of man to transform him into a Godly person in his conceptions, emotions, and behavior by altering his thoughts,

feelings, and will as well as the whole of his being. . . . It also shakes up the structure of the society and alters its inherited beliefs, well-established traditions, moral
conventions and prevailing systems. This cannot be achieved without wisdom and
amicability.[50]

Furthermore, some activist scholars argue that extremism is a misunder-
standing of Islam, and that people who advocate violence wrongly interpret the
scriptures: "error is committed by the misguided thinking on the legitimacy of
the Holy War."[51] For example, a leading member of the Muslim Brotherhood has
argued that extremists who brand other muslims as *kafir* or apostates—such as
rulers who have not applied *shari'a* or those who follow them—are often mis-
taken on theological grounds. "Shari'a teaches that those who embrace Islam
with certainty of mind can only be expelled from its fold by proven and sub-
stantiated evidence. . . . All the obscure and vague evidence on which the extremists base their accusations are refuted by fundamental and categorical texts
in both the Quran and Sunnah."[52]

Similarly, nonactivist religious figures have been very critical of extremism.
A leading Egyptian cleric, the Shaykh al-Azhar,[53] expressed his strong opposition to the use of violence in a public rebuttal of *The Neglected Duty*.[54] Although
sympathetic to their goals, the Shaykh lamented Islamic Jihad's indifference to
the indiscriminate suffering and death that result from their tactics. "If all
Muslims who have cooperated in the building of modern Egypt—a state . . . *The
Neglected Duty* describes as 'not Islamic'—are potentially apostates and deserve to die, where will the killing stop?"[55] It is better, he says, that reformers
show restraint. "In the long run, the formation of an Islamic society is better
served by patience and persuasion than by the use of force. A group like Islamic
Jihad that acts on the argument of *The Neglected Duty* may even find itself
charged with injustice, should its activities bring harm to people regarded by
ordinary Muslims as innocent."[56]

Islamic Activism and Politics: Three Patterns

The case studies examined in the Institute discussion series illustrate three ways
in which Islamic activists have managed or responded to political order.[57] The
first is to achieve or to come near to achieving *revolutionary ascendancy*. Of
the cases considered, Iran is the clearest example of this; although Sudan was
not included in the series, it is partially comparable. In these two instances,
Islamic activists—followers of the Shi'i tradition in Iran and the Sunni tradition
in Sudan—have been able, by revolutionary means, either to monopolize

political and legal control, as in the case of Iran, or to mount a convincing effort in that direction, as in the case of Sudan (where the attempt to gain complete control of the government is still being contested in an ongoing civil war). The emphasis in this approach is on *revolutionary* ascendancy, which implies the attainment of power by nondemocratic means, typically involving the use of force.

The second approach of Islamic activists is *revolutionary resistance* to a given regime. Of the cases studied, the disruptive and frequently violent actions of Islamic activists such as those associated with the GIA in Algeria or with Hamas in the territory controlled by the Palestinian Authority (PA) (and, by extension, in Israel) offer obvious examples of this approach. The antigovernment behavior of extremist groups in Egypt might also be mentioned. In contrast to revolutionary ascendancy, the crucial variable here is the existence of an entrenched regime that is perceived as opposing inalterably the ideals and objectives of Islamic activism. Precisely because the regime is considered to be so antagonistic and so entrenched, it is concluded that extreme (nondemocratic and usually violent) measures are unavoidable.

The third response of Islamic activists to political order is *accommodation*. There are obvious illustrations of this approach in the cases of Jordan, Pakistan, Indonesia, and Turkey, although there may also be a similar tendency on the part of breakaway members of Hamas in the Palestinian territory, a portion of the Islamic Salvation Front (FIS) in Algeria, and the Muslim Brotherhood in Egypt.

The most salient index of accommodation is the willingness to accept and abide by established political rules and procedures, even though such rules deviate from the ideal standards associated with what is perceived to be the proper interpretation of Islam. In the cases of Jordan, Pakistan, and Turkey, the established system to which accommodation is made is relatively democratic. In the case of Indonesia, the system is best described as a minimally democratic form of authoritarianism.

Two additional considerations for policymakers must be noted in regard to this typology. First, a question crosscutting all three categories is whether a given expression of Islamic activism is internationally oriented or primarily local or domestic in character. In the ascendancy category, both Iran and Sudan engage in a certain degree of "international outreach." Similarly, the Palestinian group Hamas, which is an example of revolutionary resistance, has clear links to supporters in the West and elsewhere. The Jama'at-i-Islami in Pakistan—an instance of accommodationism—has sister parties in India, Bangladesh, and Kashmir, although the connections are not uniformly close. By most accounts, the Muslim Brothers in Jordan and the FIS in Algeria are essentially of domestic origin, even if they receive some funding or are otherwise influenced from outside the country.

The second consideration is that these three categories are simply reference points for analyzing the different forms of response to political order by Islamic activists. There is nothing fixed about a group's position in regard to the categories. Given constituencies may move from one category to another depending on the circumstances; equally, as the section on Jordan and the Palestinians illustrates, the orientation of particular groups may shift as the demographics change and a different generation of activists with different ideas of political action takes control. Similarly, the international orientation of the groups within these categories is fluid.

Consequently, the fact that at a given time and place a particular group of Islamic activists appears to be in one category or another does not of itself resolve the controversy between those who believe Islamic activism is essentially antidemocratic, and those who think of it as being much more adaptable. Proper analysis requires more than categorization. It also requires in-depth diagnosis and careful prognostication, which involve inspecting and assessing the intentions, capabilities, and opportunities of a given group under particular conditions. If members of the FIS of Algeria currently talk like accommodationists, can they be trusted? Are they in fact becoming more moderate? Is the group unified and disciplined in accord with a given set of intentions and objectives, or is it made up of conflicting factions pulling in different directions? Is it possible that moderation might give way to extremism, or that extremists may become moderate? Under what conditions would such changes likely occur? In short, the categories serve a purpose, but they by no means obviate the need for astute analysis and projection based on an examination of specific circumstances.

POLICY IMPLICATIONS

U.S. Foreign Policy

In practice, both the Bush and the Clinton administrations have sought to distinguish between moderate political opposition and militant extremism. U.S. policy is committed both to containing extremism and to addressing its causes.

In that way, policymakers seek to balance concern about economic and political reform with the needs of local and regional stability. Put simply, U.S. policy seeks to "actively contain those states and organizations which promote or support religious or secular extremism; and help form a community of like-minded Middle Eastern states which share our goals of free markets [and] democratic enlargement."[58]

Both administrations have repeatedly stated their commitment to open political systems, human rights, and economic development as key features of their policies in the Islamic world. Increasing political participation is considered to be the best means of ensuring civil liberties and political accountability. The Clinton administration, in particular, has preferred "constructive engagement" to confrontation, and negotiation to military solutions. High priority has been given to economic policy—ending the Arab boycott against Israel and opening trade throughout the Islamic world—as a means of addressing widespread poverty. "It is in large part the lack of economic, educational, and political opportunities that gives extremists of any sort their constituency. The viable, long-term means to defeat extremism is to address the conditions on which it thrives."[59]

Simultaneously, the Clinton administration has actively sought to contain militant extremism. This includes the imposition of a trade and investment embargo against Iran in response to that country's support of terrorism in the Middle East and elsewhere. In North Africa, "the United States is seeking to build a regional bulwark against Algeria's radical Islamic insurgency."[60] The United States also remains a significant partner in long-standing bilateral and multilateral security arrangements in the Islamic world, particularly in the Gulf region, where the United States maintains a large naval presence and where it intervened on behalf of Kuwait in the 1991 Gulf War. Collective security arrangements and arms sales to U.S. allies are designed to minimize the challenge of militant groups to existing regimes. Support for the Middle East peace process is meant to further isolate extremists by providing incentives for moderation.

Critics of the Clinton administration policy claim that while the rhetoric is good, the implementation has been inconsistent.[61] It is asserted that the tendency to overlook human rights abuses and harassment of political opposition by U.S. allies such as Saudi Arabia and Egypt is not in accord with the positions articulated by policymakers.[62] Similarly, the Bush administration's failure to condemn the Algerian military for interceding in the December 1991 elections raised questions about American impartiality and its commitment to democratic norms.[63] U.S. policy in Turkey, Pakistan, Indonesia, and other countries is similarly confronted by criticisms of inconsistency in regard to human rights norms.

These criticisms reflect attempts by policymakers to strike a balance between the often-competing goals of long-term democratic development, on the one hand, and short-term regional stability, on the other. Political and economic reform can be destabilizing, and open elections may bring to power Islamic activists who have no more commitment to democracy and human rights than the regimes they seek to replace.[64] Western support for democratization is therefore complicated by "those who would use the democratic process to come to power, only to destroy that process in order to retain power and political dominance."[65]

Short-term economic and strategic interests are similarly at odds with the longer-term goals of democratization. Particularly in the Gulf and the Middle East, U.S. national security interests are dominated by access to the region's energy resources and by U.S. commitments to Israeli security. Regional stability and a Middle East peace settlement are integrally linked to these two overarching interests. Efforts to secure such short-term interests, however, often come at the expense of the long-term goals of political and economic security. Political repression by U.S. allies in the region, while ensuring stability and containing opposition to the peace process, erodes the foundations upon which future democratic societies can be built. The question, then, is should Western policymakers push for "more democratic, open regimes, even if they are likely to bring instability or even adversarial Islamic regimes? Or should they be silent in the face of increasingly authoritarian regimes that fail to address underlying issues but which nonetheless assure an enforced stability?"[66]

A dramatic example of this dilemma is Egypt. One of America's key allies in the region, Egypt has played a major role in facilitating the Middle East peace process and normalizing relations between Israel and many of its neighbors. At the same time, Egypt is plagued by serious social and economic problems, and the current government of President Hosni Mubarak has been challenged by militant activists operating within Egypt's borders. They have killed police, civilians, and foreign tourists, and have posed a serious threat to the state. In the past several years, President Mubarak has retaliated with an aggressive and highly controversial campaign involving irregular enforcement measures, military courts, and emergency legislation. While the crackdown is justified in the name of combating extremism, opposition forces of all sorts have been targeted, including accommodationist elements among the Muslim Brothers and labor leaders identified with the movement.

Commentators differ on the lesson to be learned from this example. Some analysts see a clear, positive lesson for U.S. policy in Mubarak's achievement: "[W]hile there have been strains between the United States and Cairo . . . , it's crucial to get the U.S.-Egyptian relationship back on track and to support Mubarak fully in his campaign against domestic terror. Egypt's future turns on Mubarak's ability to keep terrorism under control. Only then will it be possible to focus on Egypt's economy."[67]

Others, however, have cast Mubarak's policy toward Islamic activism in a less positive light. If militants have been subdued, "the cost has been high in terms of abuses such as torture, extra-judicial killings, imprisonment without trial and mass arrests in villages suspected of harboring militants."[68] Since the social and economic situation in Egypt continues to pose a serious challenge to the Egyptian leadership, the question remains whether the long-term prospects for Egypt are better than before the crackdowns. The manifestation of discontent may have been curtailed, but the underlying causes remain, and, consequently, Egypt remains susceptible to extremist agitation.

The situation in Egypt also typifies the dilemmas inherent within examples of revolutionary resistance, such as Algeria. There, as in Egypt, it appears that the ruling regime's hard-line response has contained the Islamist challenge, yet the underlying problems on which extremists have capitalized remain. In both of these cases, the Clinton administration has dealt with this dilemma by supporting a policy of quiet dialogue. The administration has pressed for gradual political and economic reform without showing much public displeasure about the use of emergency policies. In each instance, more immediate foreign policy concerns[69] have taken priority over longer-term goals. The question remains, however, whether short-term repression is at all compatible with long-term liberalization.

In examples of revolutionary ascendancy, such as Iran, U.S. policy faces a different set of dilemmas. American efforts to isolate Iran have been hindered by the European and Japanese policy of "constructive engagement." Fundamentally, the United States, Europeans, and Japanese differ in their interpretations of the Iranian leadership; these differences in turn produce conflicting policies. The U.S. policy of "containment"—which includes economic embargoes and political pressure—is based on a perception of Iran as a renegade state dominated by extremists. European and Japanese policies, however, seek to cultivate what they see as pragmatic elements within the Iranian leadership through strengthened trade relations. Precisely because the Iranian leadership does appear to have both pragmatic and extremist elements, neither the U.S., European, nor Japanese approaches is perceived as entirely effective. The U.S. policy of containment is argued to be overly punitive and, ultimately, counterproductive. Constructive engagement, however, is said to be too permissive, and does not hold Iran accountable for nuclear proliferation or for its direct support of militant groups, among other issues.

Accommodationist forms of Islamic activism are not without their policy dilemmas either. In the case of Pakistan, the fact that an activist organization like the Jama'at-i-Islami has been permitted to participate in the political system has, it appears, been successful in deterring extremism. The inclusion of the Jama'at in the political process has both mitigated its ideological demands and shaped its largely accommodationist methods. Dedicated Islamic reformists, who might otherwise have turned to revolutionary means, have adjusted themselves to the rules of peaceful compromise and coalition building. "It is really quite incredible the degree to which Jama'at-i-Islami has not only become part of the system but has been co-opted and used by various regimes."[70]

At the same time, it is not clear that Jama'at's participation has invariably contributed to the advance of democracy and tolerance in Pakistan, or that political experience has helped to liberalize its ideals. At the behest of the Jama'at, controversial Islamic laws were passed during the administration of President Zia-ul-Haq that manifest little regard for the rights of minorities or religious dissenters.[71] Likewise, in Indonesia, President Suharto's policy of accommodating, if not co-opting, Islam has led to the Islamization or "greening" of political discourse. Although this has allowed a flowering of Islamic modernist thought, there is serious concern that the politicization of religion is increasing communal tensions, eroding the country's tradition of tolerance, and moving it in an extremist direction. It is not clear, then, whether policies of accommodation necessarily produce democracy. In some cases, they may actually hinder it.

The Civil Society Option

Some analysts contend that the best way to coordinate the urgent imperative of deterring extremism with the ideals of equity and moderation is to cultivate something known as "civil society." Civil society is broadly understood as that sector of social life that lies beyond direct governmental administration and forms the basis of a pluralist and open society. The institutions of civil society typically include nongovernmental organizations such as trade unions, professional associations, civic groups, religious organizations, private educational institutions, and an independent media. Although autonomous, civil society is governed by the rule of law; it is also characterized by civility, tolerance of dissenting views, and accountable government, all of which serve as a buffer against both the oppression of authoritarian rule and the intolerance of extremist ideologies.

Judith Miller of the *New York Times*, among others, has supported the idea of civil society as an alternative for U.S. policymakers. She argues that the United States needs to avoid equating democracy with elections and should instead press more strongly for adherence by all sides to international standards of human rights and greater public participation within society. In regard to the situation in Algeria, she notes the following:

> The Bush Administration should have said that America would promote elections tomorrow and civil society today—increased participation in public life by a growing number of individuals, groups, and associations who genuinely crave liberal democracy—so that the concepts and traditions upon which democracy depends have time to take root, and so that countries that have known little else but one-party authoritarian rule will stand a better chance of developing truly democratic governments. . . . [The Bush administration] should have stressed . . . modest goals: increased political participation in government and the need for a freer press and freer public debate in all countries in the region.[72]

Fostering civil society is, according to Miller, a more realistic way of advancing U.S. ideals and interests than is advocating wholesale political and legal renovation. Reform is gradual and piecemeal, rather than abrupt and systemic. Freedom of the press is developed over time, and professional and social welfare organizations are promoted, all of which work cumulatively to strengthen the moderate center and to isolate extremism.

Moreover, it is argued that the idea of civil society is adaptable. However Western its roots, civil society is not a matter of replicating Western institutions; rather, this approach would, ideally, allow for indigenous forms of responsive government and public participation. John Esposito of Georgetown University notes that "Islamist movements have themselves done a great deal to promote the evolution of civil society. The Egyptian professional syndicates, especially those dominated by the Muslim Brotherhood, such as the Lawyers' Syndicate, . . . have been among the most democratic and pluralist institutions within that society."[73]

Turkey is cited as an example of a country where a vibrant civil society has formed the basis of a functioning democracy. Turkey's independent judiciary, moderately free press, and opposition political parties (including the Islamic Refah party) all provide legitimate outlets for dissent. The Turkish military, essentially controlled by the civilian government, also serves to remind the politicians that policies must remain within certain bounds. These institutions serve as "shock absorbers" that protect the country from extreme political swings and provide the mediating institutions that mitigate extremism. If there is a danger in Turkey, it is not the Islamic activists per se, but, rather, the current economic and political problems that threaten the country's continued development.

Although some observers contend that the features of civil society "do not fully apply in Arab culture as they do in the West,"[74] the notions of political representation and accountability are quite consistent with the Islamic concepts of consensus (*ijma*) and consultation (*shura*). Similarly, the Islamic emphasis on justice and law would appear to demand government accountability and greater respect for the rule of law, which are both key components of civil society. Finally, nonstate associations and private commerce are not alien to the Islamic tradition, nor are the ideals of tolerance and civility, even if their appearance in political discourse is often lacking.

There are some difficulties, however, with this concept. Hamas, for example, qualifies as a member of civil society because of its nongovernmental status and its voluntary commitment to improving the welfare of the people. It remains unclear, however, whether the group's ideology and objectives work to encourage the degree of diversity, tolerance, and freedom of expression upon which civil society—wherever it occurs—would appear to depend. There are similar uncertainties about other expressions of Islamic activism.

The real issue is not whether civil society is consistent with Islam but, rather, whether Islamic activists and other Muslims can find ways to interpret their tradition in ways that affirm the essentials of civil society, specifically the conditions of political and religious tolerance. Tolerance is not about uniformity of opinion; it is about forbearance in the face of disagreement. At a minimum, tolerance is the capacity "to respond to beliefs and practices regarded as deviant or objectionable without forcible interference." It seems that the absence of this capacity, when confronted with opposition and dissent, is a major cause of political repression and polarization. An important step toward overcoming social conflict would therefore appear to be developing a political culture that does not equate dissent with either treason or heresy. "Civil society is more than an admixture of various forms of association, it also refers to a quality—civility—without which the [political] milieu [of society] consists of feuding factions, cliques and cabals. . . . [I]t is . . . a cast of mind, a willingness to live and let live."[75]

CONCLUSION

The task of making policy in regard to Islamic activism varies, it seems, from place to place and case to case. There was little criticism in the Institute discussion series of the official statements of general policy of either the Bush or the Clinton administrations. The problems therefore arise not in stating goals, but in putting them into practice in concrete circumstances.

Although stated policy—and the cases examined by the Institute working group—affirms the division among activists between moderates and extremists, the implications are not entirely clear. Although it does appear to be the case that incentives for moderation do work toward accomplishing the limited goal of deterring extremism, it remains uncertain whether a policy of accommodation necessarily leads to greater stability and democracy. It is difficult to gauge the depth of commitment to moderation among those activists who at any given time are ready to accommodate to existing regimes. Conversely, efforts by allied regimes to "eradicate" Islamic extremists often go too far and justify the repression of all political opposition, whether religious or secular, moderate or militant. Such policies neither resolve the underlying issues that fuel extremism nor ensure the stability and long-term security that is so desperately sought.

One alternative approach to these issues, the so-called civil society option, seeks to achieve the stated goals of U.S. policy by encouraging a process of gradual economic and political reform within individual countries. According to this recommendation, room must be made for free expression and for the expansion of nongovernmental, civilly committed organizations. This demands, first, that opposition political groups willing to play by the rules be tolerated, regardless of whether they are Islamic or secular. Second, it requires that these same groups forsake the use of violence, accept the rule of law, and tolerate—by their actions and words—existing regimes.[76]

For U.S. policymakers, this type of approach—pressing for economic and political reform in a gradual manner—may be the answer to the central dilemma of balancing long-term goals with short-term interests. Although specific reforms must be developed internally, there is a role for U.S. policymakers to encourage and facilitate the necessary reforms. Because of the diversity of the Islamic world, translating these ideas and policies into operational terms and finding that balance where reform can be pursued without endangering the ultimate goal will have to be done on a case-by-case basis. The remainder of this report examines specific cases within the context of these ideas and themes.

1

IRAN

C laims that the Iranian revolution is dead and that it has lost its popular appeal are based on widespread domestic discontent with the ruling clerics and the failed expectations of the revolutionary regime. Such discontent is exacerbated by the country's extremely poor economic performance and continuing political repression. What little legitimacy the regime is able to maintain derives from its appeal to the Islamic ideology that helped bring it to power in 1979. Without this foundation and without the demon of the West—especially the United States—to distract a domestic constituency, many experts feel that the Islamic regime in Iran would collapse.

There remain, consequently, individuals within the Iranian regime who actively perpetuate a state of tension with the West in order to maintain a tenuous grip on power. Such policies, however, work against what many see as the country's basic interests; for Iran to revive its ailing economy and to address the practical needs of the country, it needs Western capital and technology.

These differing perceptions of interests are reflected within the Iranian government. There is a division between those who support a pragmatic course in international relations and those who cling to a vision of Iran as the standard bearer of revolutionary Islam throughout the world. These ideological and pragmatic tendencies often work at cross-purposes, making Iranian foreign policy inconsistent; they also make U.S. policy toward Iran difficult to formulate since neither tendency seems dominant. As Shaul Bakhash argued, "Iran's foreign policy is driven by, and is best understood as, the result of a dialectic, or a tension, between pragmatic and ideological considerations."[1]

In his presentation to the Institute working group, Bakhash noted that the pragmatists within Iran seek to stabilize the economy, secure technology, develop trade links abroad, and maintain stable and secure borders. Led by

Speaker Rafsanjani, such pragmatists have sought to rationalize exchange rates, secure foreign lending, and privatize economic assets, all in an effort to address the issues facing a troubled economy. It was this same group that helped bring about a cease-fire ending the Iran-Iraq war, and that worked to normalize relations with the United Kingdom and France. The pragmatists also worked to resume diplomatic ties with Saudi Arabia, Egypt, and Jordan. Bakhash further argued that during the Gulf War, Iran "for all intents and purposes, aligned itself with the aims of the U.S.-led alliance."[2]

The efforts by such pragmatists to work constructively within the international community are at odds, however, with a self-image of the Iranian regime as the ideological leader of a worldwide Islamic awakening. This image—rooted in the regime's revolutionary past—is colored by an anticolonial rhetoric and by a Manichean sense of the universe that sees the revolutionaries of Iran engaged in a pitched battle with the capitalist powers of the West, the so-called world devourers. Islam, from this perspective, is the advocate of the downtrodden in the world, and a tool to be used against both capitalist exploitation and communist atheism. Islam is seen by the Iranian clerics as a means of liberation, in both a spiritual and a material sense. The perceived universality of this message "impels Iran's leaders to support Islamic movements and to project the Iranian revolution outside Iran's borders."[3]

This "revolutionary dynamic" within Iran remains the most significant stumbling block to the country's normalization of relations with the West. While all revolutions are ultimately about power, they generally—and the Iranian revolution in particular—need ideals to provide legitimacy.[4] For the ruling clerics to take steps toward accommodation with their ideologically defined enemy means losing what little legitimacy the regime maintains. Having lost the support of the populace and, to a large extent, that of the traditional religious establishment, the one thing the regime retains is its revolutionary ideology. To compromise would mean, effectively, the end of the revolution, and with it the claim to unchallenged power.

U.S., EUROPEAN, AND JAPANESE POLICIES

The U.S., European, and Japanese governments have divergent views about the Iranian regime, reflecting the dichotomy within Iran itself; these differences, in turn, produce conflicting policies toward the regime. The United States has seen Iran as an outlaw or "renegade" state since the revolution in 1979 and has sought to isolate the ruling regime through economic embargoes and political pressure. Europe and Japan, however, have tended to overlook Iran's ideological tendencies and have followed a policy of "constructive engagement." This policy of engagement caters to the pragmatic tendency within Iran's leadership by seeking to integrate Iran into the community of nations through economic and political ties. It is felt that more normal relations will result from engaging Iran and opening the country to outside forces such as modern media communications, ideas, and trade.

Unfortunately, many feel that neither of these approaches has achieved its goals. Criticism of the U.S. policy of containment is based on the charge that containment has been ineffective and even self-defeating. The policy is argued to be ineffective because the U.S. economic embargo of Iran is undermined by the European and Japanese firms that continue to do business with the revolutionary regime. It is also seen as self-defeating since the policies designed to isolate Iran may in fact strengthen the extremists internally and bolster the regime's standing among developing nations. These policies are said to give reality to the regime's characterization of the United States as the "great Satan," and to justify the government's continued authoritarian policies by allowing it to portray a sense of victimization.

While some criticize the policy of containment, others argue that the policy of engagement is flawed in that it does nothing to hold Iran accountable for actions that are inconsistent with international law. Such a passive attitude, it is argued, exacts no price for Iran's financial support of militant groups (such as Hizbullah in Lebanon and Hamas in the West Bank and Gaza) or for such regime-sponsored actions as assassinating Iranian nationals on European soil. From this perspective, European and Japanese policies not only indulge the regime but also provide Iran with the financial resources to carry out its activities. Finally, it is argued that "constructive engagement" is more rhetoric than reality, and that Europe and Japan are driven largely by commercial interests.

The ability of the United States to pressure Europe and Japan into taking a harder line with Iran was weakened for some time by the failure of U.S. companies to discontinue doing business with Iran. Until June 1995, American companies such as Exxon, Mobil, Coastal, Chevron, and Texaco bought a significant percentage of Iran's oil exports, although they refined and sold the oil in other countries because of a prohibition on U.S. companies importing Iranian oil in to the United States.[5] In 1994, this amounted to 30 percent of Iran's oil exports, providing Iran with $4.25 billion in revenue and making the United States one of Iran's largest trading partners. The Clinton administration has since established an embargo on all trade and investment in Iran, precluding U.S. companies from purchasing Iranian oil or exporting into Iran.[6] The administration has also signed into law legislation that imposes sanctions on any company that knowingly finances investments of more than $40 million a year to develop the petroleum resources of Iran.[7]

A final criticism raised by the Institute working group is the perceived confusion about the ultimate ends of U.S. policy. Although Clinton administration officials have been careful to define their goal as the moderation of Iranian behavior,[8] there still appears to be a perception that the government's true intention is to overthrow the revolutionary regime. Speaker of the U.S. House of Representatives, Newt Gingrich, stated that "replacement of the current regime in Iran [is] the only long-range solution that makes any sense."[9] This statement, coupled with a House vote to provide $20 million for covert actions against Iran, seems to reinforce Iranian perceptions of U.S. intractability. As one participant noted, "U.S. policy as stated seems as if it is fundamentally hostile to Iran—not just the mullahs—and that anything they do will not be enough."[10]

If the policies of "isolation" and of "indulgence" are both flawed, what are the alternatives? The Institute working group discussed several approaches, most of which sought to link "carrots" and "sticks" much more closely to Iranian actions. One such idea was to tie funding from the International Monetary Fund (IMF) to behavior in accord with international norms, thus establishing a system of inducements that would provide positive or negative responses to specific activities.[11] Although some argued that the IMF may not be the most appropriate vehicle, the participants did agree that the underlying idea of tying incentives to action is sound. An alternative approach might be to set up a United Nations development project with Iran to provide economic assistance and help establish regional security relationships.[12] Such a multilateral mechanism would engage Iran and provide inducements for "good behavior," while also being able to withhold benefits in response to violations of international law.[13] The role of the United Nations in ending the Iran-Iraq war makes it uniquely able to carry out this type of project.

Two other related alternatives were raised during the Institute meetings. The first would couple military containment with political and economic engagement, similar to U.S. policy toward the former Soviet Union. This approach assumes that, although the regime may not be ready to engage the West, Iranian society is. Cultivating commercial relations with the local businessmen—the merchants of the bazaar—is perceived to be an effective way to engage Iranian society at the local level and to begin opening the country to outside influences. The second alternative similarly encourages some form of engagement—in this case, low-level diplomatic engagement—and cultivation of person-to-person contacts. Although this approach would maintain the economic embargo, it would seek to develop a second track of engagement, that of quiet diplomacy. This alternative takes a different view of containment: although imperfect, containment has had considerable success. The sanctions have achieved limited goals, such as inhibiting the regime's ability to support militant activities by denying it the financial means to do so. Such pressure should therefore not be removed without some change in Iranian behavior.

Two key issues remain, however, for Western policymakers. The first is to decide whether revolutionary Iran *should* be integrated into the international community and, second, whether it *can* be integrated. As the previous discussion indicates, the first issue elicits different responses from different countries. While there was some consensus about reviewing current policy and exploring some form of engagement, the workshop participants recognized the political limitations on any significant change in light of U.S. history with Iran. Both the 1979 revolution and the Iran-Contra scandal continue to haunt U.S.-Iranian relations. While some may be uncomfortable with the existing approach, it is unlikely, politically, that a new one will emerge.

As to the second issue, policymakers need to recognize the limited ability of (or desirability for) the United States or other countries to influence the internal dynamics of the regime. As one participant noted, Reagan administration attempts to do just that ended in disaster. The success of any policy to encourage moderation depends on the Iranian response—and there was little optimism among the working group participants about securing a positive reaction from the regime in Tehran. Nor is there much evidence to indicate that domestic support exists within Iran for a rapprochement with the West. Earlier attempts by Rafsanjani and others to pursue a policy of accommodation—including Iran's neutrality during the Gulf War and its efforts to facilitate the release of Western hostages in Lebanon—were seen as unsuccessful and have since been discredited within the regime.[14] Besides, as previously noted, the ideological and political dynamics within Iran remain a serious obstacle to the normalization of relations, even if the regime wanted to pursue such a policy.

PRIMARY CONSIDERATIONS

The three dominant concerns of U.S. policymakers are Iran's efforts to acquire weapons of mass destruction (particularly nuclear weapons), its continuing financial support of extremist groups engaged in political violence, and its opposition to the Middle East peace process. Movement by Iran in these three areas is considered to be a prerequisite for a normalization of relations with the United States.

Iran has been engaged in a military buildup since the end of the Iran-Iraq war in an effort to establish its position as a regional power.[15] This includes the purchase of Russian submarines and aircraft, Chinese missiles, and chemical weapons materials. Even more ominous is the transfer of nuclear technology and advisers from both Russia and China to Iran. The agreement between Iran and Russia to build a two-reactor power plant and to train a new generation of Iranian engineers, coupled with the Chinese agreement to build two other reactors and similarly to transfer expertise,[16] significantly increases Iran's ability to produce nuclear weapons. Although Iranian officials deny any intention to develop nuclear weapons, the Israeli government notified the United States last fall of intelligence reports that "Iran was actively seeking the capability to make nuclear fuel that could be used in a crude explosive device."[17] Furthermore, U.S. officials have noted that it is unlikely that a country with the oil and natural gas resources of Iran would need nuclear power for civilian purposes.[18]

The current administration's containment policy has actively sought to limit Iran's developing military capabilities. First, the Clinton administration has tried to block the transfer of sensitive technologies to Iran through multilateral agreements and strict export controls. Second, the administration has attempted to hinder Iran's economic ability to purchase advanced technologies by maintaining economic sanctions on the country. While there remains disagreement over these sanctions, a large number of countries concur on the need to prohibit exports of advanced weapons technology to Iran, with Russia and China being notable exceptions to this consensus.

Iran's continuing support for extremist groups heightens the concern over how Tehran would use nuclear and missile capability. The revolutionary regime in Iran "has demonstrably utilized a variety of means, including supply of money and arms, hostage-taking, terrorism, and—in the case of Iranian dissidents abroad—assassination, to advance its policy aims."[19] It is said to have funded and trained the Hamas suicide bombers in order to undermine the Middle East peace process.[20] The regime also provides funding and arms to Lebanon's

Hizbullah, the Sudanese National Islamic Front, Algerian Islamic groups, and other extremist groups.

Despite Iran's willingness to engage in terrorism to achieve its goals, it is cautious in its relations with certain countries it deems of value to the projection of its influence abroad. As Bakhash noted, Iran has pursued a policy of "selective radicalism," being careful not to antagonize Europe and Japan or to destabilize the countries on its immediate borders. Iran has not taken an active role in support of Muslims in Chechnya, Tajikistan, or other Central Asian nations for fear of destabilizing the region in which it lives or of provoking a response from Russia. Rather, Iran has reserved most of its activism for countries farther away, such as Lebanon, Bosnia, Sudan, and Algeria.[21]

Iran's activities can be explained to some degree by the regime's sense of isolation and its fear of "encirclement" by hostile countries. Supporting Islamic movements around the world, aside from the ideological motivation, is seen by the regime as enhancing its own security by strengthening friendly constituencies in the Muslim world, and perhaps creating future regimes sympathetic to its cause. Similarly, Iran's effort to accumulate modern weaponry is fueled by the harsh lessons learned in its war with Iraq of falling behind technologically in a regional arms race. It is also linked to Iran's ambitions and desire for regional hegemony, and to Saudi Arabia's acquisition of sophisticated weaponry from the United States.

These activities, however threatening, are not unique in the region. Syria and Libya have long supported militant groups, Saudi Arabia continues to be a source of funding for Islamic activism in many countries, and Iraq—along with most nations in the region—has spent considerable amounts of money developing its military capabilities. What makes Iran different is the direct link between these activities and the regime's religious claims to paramountcy. "Iran may be responsible for less state terrorism than Syria and less missionary mischief than Saudi Arabia, but al-Assad's Syria and King Fahd's Saudi Arabia are not self-proclaimed millenarian beacons to the Muslim Third World."[22]

It is the religious or ideological dimension coupled with the destabilizing role that Iran has defined for itself that distinguishes the regime and makes Western dealings with the government particularly difficult. As previously noted, the propaganda dimension of Iran's revolution remains extremely important to the regime. From a tactical perspective, the revolutionary rhetoric is perceived as helping the regime "coalesc[e] Islamic forces in a powerful tide against the U.S. and Iran's other rivals and enemies."[23] Such propaganda remains influential because there are those who believe it. Many of Iran's leaders feel that they are "competing for the hearts and minds of Muslims worldwide against various claimants: the corrupting attractions of Western culture, secularists of all stripes, and other activist Islamic states like Saudi Arabia."[24] Because of this dedication, many people in Iran remain deeply committed to the ideal of an Islamic state insulated from the corrupting influence and temptations of Western culture.

Questions persist, however, about how potent Iran's messianism really is. As Shaul Bakhash noted, there is an odd mix of triumphalism and defeatism within the Iranian leadership itself. "On the one hand, the Islamic tide seems irreversible."[25] The examples of Iran itself, the establishment of an Islamic regime in Sudan, and the effectiveness of different movements such as Hizbullah and Hamas all appear to testify to the strength of Islam as an alternative ideology for the world. "On the other hand, Iran's leaders look around and seem to see nothing but doom and gloom."[26] The collapse of the former Soviet Union and the increased influence of the United States and other Western countries, the Gulf War, the disunity among the Muslim nations of the world, and the apparent success of the Middle East peace process all testify—in Iranian eyes—to the inherent vulnerability of Islam in the world.

The effect of these contradictory perceptions concerning Islamic influence is similarly reflected in questions about Iran's leadership. It is clear that much of the Muslim world does not affirm the image of Iran as the center of a worldwide Islamic revival. According to one participant, the assumption that Iran is the preeminent Islamic state is accepted nowhere besides Iran, and even there only among its leaders.[27] Furthermore, there is criticism from within Iran's religious structure itself that the regime is giving Islam a bad name and that it is fueling anticlericalism—a previously unknown phenomenon in Iran.

Nonetheless, Iran does continue to have an impact in countries throughout the developing world precisely because of its religious rhetoric and its appeals to Islam.[28] Regardless of the situation within Iran, the ideal of an Islamic revolution remains potent; the perception of the Iranian brand of Islam as "the hope of the world's disinherited" strongly resonates among disaffected populations throughout the Muslim world.

2

ALGERIA

lgeria has been plagued by civil strife since 1992, when its armed forces intervened in parliamentary elections and established a military government. The Islamic Salvation Front (FIS)—a coalition of Islamic activists—was then poised to win a decisive majority in a second round of balloting, and would have been the first Islamic opposition group to come to power through popular referendum anywhere. The elections, however, were suspended, the FIS leadership arrested, and the party banned. As justification, the military leadership argued that had the FIS been allowed to take power, democracy would have been short-lived; the elections would have been "one man, one vote, one time."

The impasse in Algeria epitomizes the dilemma faced by Western policymakers seeking both democratic development and regional stability. While the ruling regime in Algeria has been demonstrably repressive, the commitment of the FIS to democratic values is also questionable. The fragmentation of the Islamic activists since 1992 has spawned several militant groups actively engaged in political violence. The response of the military has been to pursue a policy of "eradication" that has exacerbated the conflict and increased the death toll. Both groups have been responsible for large numbers of civilian deaths. As William Zartman of Johns Hopkins University remarked, "In Algeria, there are no good guys."[1]

A great deal has changed since 1992, and since the Institute meeting in the fall of 1994. The ruling regime has been able to contain the Islamic opposition, stabilize its rule, and successfully hold presidential elections. Yet Algeria remains very much divided, and underlying economic, social, and political problems persist. How Algeria deals with these more intractable issues will provide a glimpse into the future of the modern Middle East, for Algeria is seen by many as an indicator of what the future holds for the region: reform and reconciliation, continued military rule, or civil war.

THE FAILED SOCIAL CONTRACT AND THE RISE OF ISLAMIC ACTIVISM

In 1962, after a bitter eight-year independence struggle, the National Liberation Front (FLN) replaced the French colonial regime that had ruled Algeria since the nineteenth century. The economic and political policies adopted by the newly established FLN government demanded personal austerity from the Algerian people in return for the promise of equality and economic development. Income from oil and gas reserves helped fund a drive toward industrialization that, it was hoped, would eventually produce a higher standard of living for all Algerians. A one-party political system dominated by the FLN developed to guide these policies, deriving its legitimacy from the party's central role in securing independence from France.

Twenty-five years later, neither the political nor the economic policies of Algeria's "state capitalism" were working. While the FLN had achieved some success in providing employment, education, and health care, the state structure fell far short of meeting the demands of a rapidly growing population. The collapse in oil prices and resulting loss of income during the early 1980s eliminated the cushion upon which FLN economic policies had long relied. The faltering economy brought to light the flaws within the political system and led to charges of corruption and mismanagement. "The growing gap between those who had no access to FLN patronage and the elite of public sector managers, party apparatchiks, and allied FLN officers exposed the true nature of the party."[2] Bread riots in October 1988 presented a serious challenge to the ruling regime.

The authoritarian rule of the FLN had also generated discontent among the population. While the 1988 riots were a protest against the FLN's failed economic policies, the absence of political accountability also inspired significant discontent. The government's use of force against the demonstrators, which left more than four hundred civilians dead, further undermined the legitimacy of the regime. To improve its standing, the government initiated reforms to liberalize the political process. These included constitutional changes that provided for the formation of political parties and for the regional and local elections held in 1990.[3] Despite the manipulation of electoral laws to ensure the FLN's success, the regime did extremely poorly in the 1990 elections.

Although Algerian opposition movements have always been colored by "the espousal of Islam and its values,"[4] it is argued that the FLN's policies contributed to the rise of Islamic activism. The dominance of one-party rule in postindependent Algeria precluded the development of viable—and legal—opposition political parties. Religious opposition groups, particularly the FIS, were able to fill this vacuum in 1990 and become the dominant vehicle for popular discontent. It was the FIS, then, that unexpectedly fared so well in the elections at the expense of the FLN. "The landslide victory of the FIS seemed to have caught the regime off guard."[5]

The FIS served as an umbrella group for the Islamic activist movement in the early 1990s. The group was split between those who sought to maintain and work within democratic institutions, and those who advocated violence to achieve their goals. These differing, and often competing, factions did share a common goal of an Algeria ruled in line with Islamic principles, though the interpretation of this ideal remained—and still remains—a matter of debate. The policies advocated by the pragmatists "differ[ed] little from the current regime's, especially in such crucial areas as economic planning,"[6] while the more radical groups sought to reshape Algerian society in accord with their own interpretation of *shari'a*. Both moderate and militant activists, however, remained united in their deep conviction that the FLN was corrupt and illegitimate, and both believed that their actions were divinely sanctioned and would ultimately succeed.

Although the electoral gains of the FIS in the 1990 regional elections were significant, it remains unclear how many of those votes were cast in positive support of the FIS and how many were used to indicate disaffection with the FLN. The working group participants differed on this issue. One group argued that the FIS support has never been strong, and that it was "only one minority group in society."[7] More voters abstained in the 1991 elections, it was noted, than actually voted for the FIS. Others, however, contended that the positive support for the FIS was underestimated, and that many who voted against the FLN in 1990 actively began to support the FIS in December 1991.[8] The strong showing in the 1991 elections, particularly among the urban poor, is said to support this point. Out of fifty-four parties participating, the FIS took 42 percent of the vote, with the FLN coming in second with 20 percent. In this context, it was argued, 42 percent is "no slim majority."[9]

The disbanding of the FIS in 1992 and the imprisonment of its leaders splintered the activists, driving many of them underground or into exile. Several militant groups emerged, including the Armed Islamic Movement (MIA) and, later, the Armed Islamic Group (GIA). The GIA is considered to be the more radical organization, and is responsible for the December 1994 Air France hijacking, the 1995 bombings in Paris, and attacks on journalists, intellectuals, and foreigners. The MIA, a collection of smaller militant factions, has since evolved into the Islamic Salvation Army (AIS), often referred to as the armed wing of the FIS. The GIA and AIS have become rivals and have advocated significantly different policies. The GIA, for example, has opposed negotiations with the government, whereas the AIS has "called for a political settlement to the conflict."[10]

Since the aborted elections in January 1992, violence by the militant activists and the security forces has brought the country to the verge of civil war. Although there are no reliable statistics, it is estimated that perhaps more than 50,000 people have been killed since 1992; these deaths have been attributed to both sides of the conflict. A 1994 Amnesty International report noted that the security forces have detained tens of thousands of people under the emergency laws, engaged in torture, and been responsible for hundreds of extrajudicial killings. This report also points out that the Islamic militants were responsible for killing hundreds of journalists, intellectuals, political officials, and others who were presumably targeted because of their opposition to the activist agenda. Of concern has been the charge that the "leaders and spokesmen of the FIS have not only failed to condemn the deliberate and arbitrary killings of civilians by the armed [extremist] groups, but they have often justified such killings."[11]

TWO PERSPECTIVES

Two schools of interpretation emerged in the Institute discussions. The two groups differed fundamentally on which they perceived to be the lesser of two evils: the government or the Islamic activists. By one account, Islamic activists were a destructive force in the country, particularly given their antidemocratic rhetoric and the disposition of the more radical groups to employ indiscriminate violence. From this view, the government has no choice but to deny them political access, and to try, where necessary, to subdue them by force. The second perspective represented in the discussion argued that, basically, the government is to blame. The long record of governmental repression, corruption, and ineffectiveness has led to the current state of affairs. Unrest will decline only if Islamic activists are given the opportunity to compete in a new democratic contest.

Pro-Government

Speaking for the first school, William Zartman articulated the merits of the existing government. Zartman argued that the long-term viability of a democratic and open Algeria must be based on existing institutions. He maintained that strengthening the rule of law and the state structures that exist apart from the political parties is crucial to the stability and development of the society. The current regime, according to Zartman, remains the best alternative for building upon existing institutions and cultivating a democratic Algeria. While the FLN may have had its problems in the past, the current regime is not as bad. Finally, because the Islamic activists seek to dismantle these structures, their exclusion is acceptable and, perhaps, necessary.

Zartman also argued that the FIS has not enjoyed the widespread support that many attribute to it. He noted that less than 25 percent of Algerians old enough to vote supported the FIS in the 1991–92 elections, and that more than 50 percent boycotted the elections altogether.[12] Furthermore, statements by FIS political leaders hostile to women's rights, minority rights, secularism, and multiparty democracy seem to undermine the idea that an activist regime would be more democratic, as do the extremism and militancy of the AIS and GIA. Finally, it was argued that there is no alternative, viable third course open to the Algerians. Other parties (such as the Berber FFS) do not have the potential to generate mass support because of their limited ethnic base.

Zartman concluded that the best hope for Algeria's future is to support the current regime in its efforts to stabilize Algerian society and strengthen those institutions and structures that would form the basis of a democratic polity. He offered several interrelated suggestions to achieve this goal. First, like all shaky regimes, this one needs to consolidate its position and broaden its base of support. It also needs to restore law and order and establish a sense of stability virtually absent since 1988. Finally, it needs to rebuild the economy and produce tangible benefits for the people. These reforms should be pursued simultaneously, with the recognition, however, that these demands often work at cross-purposes. This is particularly true of economic reform, an area in which Western aid can have the most constructive impact.

Pro-Democracy

Critics of the pro-government position point to the perceived weakness of the existing government and note that "spent systems . . . [cannot] endure nor be propped up indefinitely."[13] According to Robin Wright of the *Los Angeles Times,* the proposal to aid the existing regime—assuming its eventual transformation—is rooted in a fallacy. The regime is charged with being incapable of dealing with the issues facing the nation; "investment in the current regime," said Wright, "is like pouring money down the drain."[14] If the current regime is bound to collapse, continued Western support for it is questionable.

The alternative to the old regime, in this view, is political pluralism. In her presentation, Wright argued that the impasse in Algeria is fundamentally not about Islam but about democracy. The Algerian people today seek freedom from repressive political rule, just as they did in their struggle for independence from France. The fact that such opposition has been articulated in religious terms simply reflects the role of Islam as the idiom of dissent. Western policymakers who focus exclusively on the militant fringe run the risk of ignoring the larger issue of political participation in the Islamic world. "A new generation of Algerian idealists, the largest number mobilized this time around an Islamic banner, is prepared to fight and die to end totalitarian military rule. . . . The global push toward empowerment and political pluralism . . . has already doomed the regime."[15]

According to this line of argument, the existing government ought to step down before it is forced out violently, and elections should be held in which all parties are able to participate. Advocates of this position further argue that U.S. support for democracy must be more than rhetorical and must recognize the results of popular elections even if the results are not in accord with U.S. interests. The alternative to a peaceful process that promotes moderation is the violent replacement of one authoritarian regime with another authoritarian regime, very likely one "whose ideology necessarily—proclaimedly—looks on the West as an enemy."[16]

DEMOCRACY, DIALOGUE, AND VIOLENCE

The two unresolved issues of this debate are, first, whether the regime is capable of reform and, second, whether the Islamic activists would support democracy if allowed to operate within an open system. There is room for doubt about the latter issue, given FIS public statements that equated democracy with heresy.[17] Furthermore, some contend that activist interpretations of *shari'a*—most notably in Sudan—are inherently undemocratic,[18] raising the larger question about the compatibility of Islamic and democratic principles.[19] Opponents of *shari'a* argue that Islamic law does not accord equal treatment to women and non-Muslims, and that it is inherently intolerant of minority religious groups. Others, however, argue that there is more than one interpretation of *shari'a*, and that there exists within Islamic tradition a strong emphasis on consensus *(ijma)* and consultation *(shura)*, which provide the foundations for a healthy democracy.

What would have happened if the FIS had come to power in 1992 cannot be known. Other Islamic activist groups have acted responsibly and "played by the rules" when allowed to participate in elections, as in Jordan, Morocco, and Kuwait. If this willingness to work within a democratic framework is real, the assumption that Islamic activism is inherently undemocratic needs to be reevaluated. Critics concede that Islamic activists have adhered to democratic principles in certain cases; however, in these instances a framework of representative institutions and laws were guaranteed by a well-established authority, such as a monarchy. This observation would imply that a necessary precursor to democracy is the development of pluralist institutions and common respect for the rule of law. Such a system is lacking in the case of Algeria.

In the context of Algeria, however, this debate is somewhat moot because it remains unclear whether either side—the current regime or its activist opposition—would readily accept the basic condition of democracy: peaceful transference of power based on electoral results. While Islamic activists can be accused of having undemocratic tendencies, the existing regime can be similarly described. For most of the last thirty years, the FLN, the state, and the government were one and the same thing; it was a system that never allowed for true power sharing.

The regime's actions since 1992 convey a mixed message about its commitment to political reform. While there are those in positions of power who appear either unwilling or unable to engage in serious political dialogue, multicandidate presidential elections were held in November 1995, and constitutional reforms were proposed in May 1996.[20] President Zeroual's victory in the 1995 election was significant, despite limited participation that resulted from both government censure and boycotts by opposition parties. The elections were seen as successful because of the large voter turnout amid threats of violence by the GIA;[21] this high turnout was perceived as "a repudiation of violence and a call for dialogue and reconciliation."[22]

The potential for future dialogue and reconciliation, however, remains uncertain. Despite the inability of either side to achieve military dominance, both the security forces and the various militant groups continue to use violence in pursuit of their goals. It is said that certain elements within the military believe that they can "eradicate" the militant movement, and impose a political solution that does not threaten the status quo. The limited success of the existing policy would seem to support this position; the military government has demonstrated a surprising resiliency and has been successful in achieving at least the immediate goal of constraining the Islamic opposition.[23] Similarly, the more extreme of the militant groups continue to refuse to negotiate with the current regime, preferring instead to use political violence to achieve their goals.[24] As one commentator noted,

> Zeroual remains shackled by the hard-line "eradicator" generals in the regime, who want no accommodation whatsoever with the Islamist opposition and no talks with the FIS. The FIS in turn is constrained by its own followers and more radical elements, such as the GIA, which it can neither persuade to lay down their arms nor afford to confront unless the regime makes some meaningful concessions.[25]

The inability of either side to make concessions for reaching some middle ground has perpetuated what many see as a "mutually hurting stalemate."[26]

The framework for a dialogue of reconciliation, however, does exist. In January 1995, the principal Algerian opposition parties met in Rome under the auspices of the Community of Sant'Egidio to sign an agreement committing the eight parties to fundamental principles of pluralism and human rights. The "Platform of National Contract" offered "a peaceful solution to the crisis by focusing on three issues: a gradual end to violence, managing a transitional period, and then democratic elections."[27] Significantly, this represented a consensus document regarding the country's future governance by a diverse group of political parties, including both the FLN (now in opposition), the FIS, and others. Notably absent, though, were government representatives. The provisions of the National Contract included (1) a specific rejection of violence either to attain or maintain power; (2) respect for human rights norms and standards; (3) "consecration of political pluralism,"[28] including the alternation of power through elections; (4) independent branches of government; and (5) the nonintervention of the army in political affairs. The ruling regime rejected the proposal shortly after its release,[29] and has since imposed restrictions on political activities inside Algeria by supporters of the Rome platform.

U.S. POLICY

The debate over U.S. policy in Algeria has tended to split between those who ardently support the regime and those who endorse some form of political settlement with the FIS. As outlined above, the latter position perceives the conflict in terms of regional democratization and sees no peace in Algeria's future without some accommodation of Islamic activism. The alternative approach specifically rejects this position and argues that the United States should wholeheartedly back its allies—France and the current Algerian regime—and drop any pretense of accommodation. It should "make clear that America stands firmly . . . against a fundamentalist takeover in Algeria."[30]

The Bush administration's slowness in condemning the military intervention in January 1992 was perceived by many as an endorsement of the "exclusionist" approach; the administration was subsequently criticized for equivocating in its support for democracy and for tacitly endorsing the military takeover. The Clinton administration's support for dialogue, however, has been criticized for promoting uncertainty in the region. Particularly controversial were meetings between State Department officials and representatives of the FIS that were held to "draw the Islamists into the political process and to help bring about a political settlement between the Algerian government and the insurgents."[31] This position was seen by some as "undercut[ing] the existing regime in Algeria" at a time when that regime had "fought the terrorists to a stalemate."[32]

Ironically, the Clinton administration's "inclusionist" approach put it at odds with France. Whereas France favors constructive engagement with Iran, it has taken a hard-line position toward Islamic activism in Algeria and "frames the conflict as a clash of civilizations."[33] The role reversal between U.S. and French foreign policy reflects the differing interests of these two countries in Algeria and in Iran. For France, the Algerian impasse is a much more immediate problem. France fears a potential influx of refugees from its former colony if an Islamic regime were to come to power. Such a situation would exacerbate existing domestic tensions in France. French enthusiasm for experiments with democracy is also limited by French reliance on Algerian fossil fuels and by the geographical proximity of Algeria. Conversely, the United States does not approach the situation with the same sense of urgency; it has sought to support— rhetorically—a long-term process of democratization and—financially—a program of economic development.[34] This approach reflects a desire to be seen as neither propping up the existing regime nor supporting militant extremism.[35]

The differences between France and the United States—or between the Bush and the Clinton administrations—over policy toward Algeria are not, however, as great as they appear, indicating that the rhetorical debate may perhaps represent a false dichotomy. "Few in Washington genuinely wanted to see the FIS succeed in toppling the regime in Algiers, just as few in Paris were confident that the 'eradicators' could prevail."[36] Administration contacts with the FIS were a pragmatic effort to avoid a repetition of what happened in Iran in 1979. In the aftermath of the 1992 elections, American policymakers were not convinced that the regime would last, and sought to maintain a neutral position in case an activist regime actually came to power. Similarly, some argue that the Bush administration's muted criticism of the military takeover in 1992 was a pragmatic response to a situation over which it had little control.

By all accounts, the Algerian regime's demonstrated staying power has altered the equation. President Zeroual's victory in the 1995 elections has strengthened the regime's legitimacy, and it appears that the regime's military policies have succeeded in marginalizing the Islamic opposition. Even though the military situation remains a stalemate, the Islamic activists are in a state of disarray. The question remains, then, whether the regime will use this opportunity to maintain the status quo or to embark on a new course. Although the economic situation has been improving, "fundamental questions of reform still need to be addressed."[37]

It is argued that there is now an opportunity for the U.S. government to influence the situation in a positive manner.[38] Such an approach is predicated upon a normalization of relations with the Algerian regime and would entail a more proactive role—in conjunction with the European allies—in Algeria, such as high-level diplomatic contacts[39] and greater economic, political, and moral support. Such a shift, however, should be linked to the regime's stated commitment to reform and reconciliation. In summary, the United States should be "more engaged with the regime and encourage it down a road it says it wants to pursue. . . . namely, a return to normal life, reform [of] the economy, [a] rebuilding [of] political institutions, parliamentary elections, and so forth. In a sense what we have to overcome is our standoffishness."[40]

Again, the principles of the Rome platform derived under the auspices of Sant'Egidio provide a framework for reform and reconciliation. The commitment to democratic principles, the rejection of violence, and respect for process provide a foundation for civility and an eventual transition to democracy. The difficulties in implementing such a change, however, remain the predominance of those who prefer a military solution to a negotiated settlement, both within the military and among the Islamic activists; "Algeria's government and its Islamic opposition [remain] divided into hard-line and accommodationist camps."[41] Western nations should review ways to facilitate or "ripen" the dialogue and to otherwise provide incentives for negotiation.

Despite efforts by the international community, however, it is argued that the effectiveness of a reconciliation process will ultimately depend on all Algerian parties accepting some form of power-sharing arrangement.[42] In countries where divided societies have undergone reconciliation—for example, South Africa, Haiti, and El Salvador—the precursor was an acceptance by the dominant political forces of a process whose end-result would be a power-sharing arrangement. The dialogue in these cases was premised on a mutual recognition that continuation of the status quo was no longer tenable for either side. It was thus perceived to be in the best interest of all concerned to work out some form of pluralistic political structure. Whether or not the current Algerian leadership or the Islamic activists have reached this point is unknown, although the message of the November 1995 electorate would indicate that the people of Algeria have.

3

JORDAN AND THE PALESTINIANS

T he Islamic movements in Jordan, the West Bank, and Gaza demonstrate the differences—and divisions—among Islamic activists. The Jordan and Palestinian Islamic movements differ in significant ways, "playing very different roles in the two polities."[1] The resort to violence by key Islamic groups based in the West Bank and Gaza is said to be linked to their marginalization from the political process. In Jordan, however, such extremism has traditionally been eschewed by the Jordanian Muslim Brotherhood, due in part to a conscious policy of inclusion. The increasingly confrontational tactics of activists throughout the region, however, has prompted Jordan, as well as Israel and the Palestinian Authority (PA), to take a more forceful position toward Islamic opposition groups, a trend that may threaten the long-term democratic development of the region.

While differences between groups are apparent, differences and tensions within groups exist as well. Although generally agreeing upon ultimate ends, differing factions have struggled with one another over how best to achieve their goals. The use of violence to achieve political ends by both the Islamic Resistance (Hamas) and the Islamic Jihad reflects the increased dominance of militants within these organizations. Such violence reflects a considered shift in tactics aimed at undermining the peace process and, subsequently, those who seek accommodation with Israel. It is argued, then, that the ultimate success or failure of the peace process will determine whether the PA or the militant extremists become the dominant voice among the Palestinians.

The U.S. response to the violence and to the challenge of Islamic activism has been to distinguish between militant extremism and popular support for social reform. The viability of separating proponents of political violence from the larger movements within which they operate—and the subsequent policy implications—is questioned by some Western scholars and analysts, as became clear in the highly contentious discussion surrounding the sensitive subject of Islamic activism in Jordan, in Israel, and in the West Bank and Gaza.

ISLAMIC MOVEMENTS IN JORDAN

The dominant Islamic movement in Jordan historically has been the Muslim Brotherhood, an offshoot of the original Brotherhood established in Egypt in 1928. Glenn Robinson argued that the Muslim Brotherhood in Jordan has had a tacit understanding with the ruling regime over the past several decades. In exchange for a somewhat protected status and an influential role in national education, the Brotherhood is said to have endorsed the Islamic claims of the regime,[2] providing it with legitimacy and limiting opposition. This has helped the Hashemite monarchy contain the secular Nasserite left as well as the more radical Islamic activists.

While the degree of actual complicity remains unclear,[3] the Brotherhood and the Hashemite monarchy have had common interests that allowed them to transcend differences in pursuit of shared objectives. The Brotherhood's "evolutionary," as opposed to revolutionary, approach to reform emphasized working within the political order and, in the late 1950s, entailed active support for the Hashemite Kingdom in opposition to leftist nationalists. "[Such] fidelity was rewarded with an exemption from the otherwise across-the-board ban on organized political activity."[4] Similarly, the Jordanian government sought to bring Islamic activists into the political process and—particularly in the 1980s—pursued a policy of co-optation: "Islamists were not to be treated as an opposition to be countered, but rather as an important interest group to be courted."[5] As a result, the Muslim Brotherhood became the "most establishment-oriented movement in the Arab world,"[6] and enjoyed a legal status that other political and religious groups in Jordan and the Middle East have not achieved.[7]

Current relations between Islamic activists and the Jordanian regime, however, have been strained, in part because of increased political pluralism. In 1989, King Hussein initiated a "preemptive"[8] process of democratization to avoid a full-scale economic and political crisis. An existing parliamentary structure was given new life, and a more pluralist political environment was created. In this new arena, Islamic candidates fared quite well, and much better than the government expected.[9] However, the open system allowed other activists to gain strength, inadvertently eliminating the Muslim Brotherhood's traditional "monopoly" as a moral authority. These independent activists have been more willing to confront the regime and question its legitimacy.

It is argued that internal changes within the Brotherhood have also had profound effects on the organization and its relation to the ruling regime. The traditional leadership of the Brotherhood was dominated by "cultural Islamists," individuals with formal religious training whose preoccupations tended to be with social issues such as the banning of alcohol and segregation of the sexes in schools. This group, traditional and conservative, supported the Hashemite monarchy. A younger generation of political activists, however, has since come to dominate the Brotherhood. It is a group more critical of the regime and of peace efforts with Israel than the older "quietist" stratum. The result has been a more confrontational approach by the Brotherhood to both Israel and the ruling Hashemite regime. The net effect has "weakened the historically strong relationship between the government and the Muslim Brotherhood."[10]

Strengthened ties between the Muslim Brotherhood in Jordan and the Islamic Resistance (Hamas) in the occupied territories have also deepened the divisions between it and the regime. Increased support by the Palestinians in Jordan for the Islamic activists has also affected the Palestinian nationalist movement. It is argued that, as a result, "today in Jordan Islamists have succeeded the PLO [Palestine Liberation Organization] as the institutional representative of Palestinians."[11] To counter the growing influence of the activists among the Palestinian section of the population, Amman has tolerated the reintroduction of secular Palestinian nationalists into Jordanian politics. This is ironic in light of "Jordan's state of perpetual tension with the PLO, the Kingdom's historic rival for the allegiance of Palestinians."[12] These developments have replicated in Jordan the secular-religious tensions characteristic of the occupied territories.

WEST BANK AND GAZA: HAMAS AND ISLAMIC JIHAD

The social forces influencing the Jordanian Muslim Brotherhood have similarly affected the Islamic activists in the occupied territories of Gaza and the West Bank. The Palestinian branch of the Muslim Brotherhood—originally linked to the Jordanian and Egyptian Muslim Brotherhoods—was characterized in the 1980s by increasing social diversity. The older, more conservative members— the traditional leadership—were drawn from the mercantile class, while the organization's grassroots supporters came largely from rural backgrounds. A third group of supporters, the so-called middle strata, tended to have urban backgrounds (many were from refugee camps), university education, and more radical views on direct action against Israeli forces.

The changing demographic realities precipitated a shift in ideology. The traditional leadership had avoided confrontation with the occupying forces, emphasizing instead spiritual liberation through a quietist strategy of recreating Palestinian society in accord with Islamic ideals. The younger, more radical members sought political liberation through confrontation with Israel, and actively opposed the leadership of the traditional conservatives. "The ideological fissures within the Islamists movement centered not on ultimate goals, as both sides wanted the establishment of an Islamic state in all of Palestine with strong ties to the larger Islamic world. Rather, the question was one of tactics: whether it was better to free the soul or the nation first."[13]

The tension between these groups came to a head during the Intifada, the popular uprising in the occupied territories that erupted in the fall of 1987. The Intifada was a continuing series of demonstrations against the occupying forces, carried out by stone-throwing youths in the streets of Gaza and the West Bank. It represented an "appropriation of political initiative"[14] by those within the occupied territories away from the PLO leadership in exile. The militant tone of the Intifada derived largely from the actions of Islamic Jihad, a militant group established in the 1980s that drew on the political experience of former members of the PLO and the Popular Front for the Liberation of Palestine (PLFP) and engaged in armed operations inside the occupied territories. The violence found support among the population in the territories, and set the stage for the active confrontation of the Intifada.[15]

For the Muslim Brotherhood, the Intifada represented a shift from quietist passivity to active confrontation. The divisions in class and ideology between the upper and middle strata of the Muslim Brotherhood led to an internal revolt over control of the organization. It was the middle strata that emerged victorious, successfully transforming the quietist Brotherhood into the Islamic Resistance Movement, known more commonly as Hamas.[16]

Goals, Violence, and Political Support

Both Islamic Jihad and Hamas have sought to overthrow Israeli rule by force, and establish an Islamic state in its place. They perceive Zionism to be an obstacle to the Islamization of society that cannot be accommodated,[17] and, consequently, have raised opposition to Israel to the level of a religious duty.[18]

While they link their religious ideology to Palestinian nationalism and to issues of social justice, they remain defined, in Western eyes, by their militancy.

The use of violence—particularly against civilian populations—has brought notoriety to Hamas and the more radical, though less influential, Islamic Jihad. The extreme tactics, in most cases, have strengthened Hamas's support among many Palestinians "who want to confront the Israeli occupiers."[19] Among these supporters, violence is seen as a legitimate matter of self-defense.[20] Such sentiments reflect a profound sense of victimization and the perceived powerlessness of the Palestinians to shape their own destiny. The resort to terror is "the most feasible and satisfying response to the . . . forces that demean modern Palestinian and Arab cultures: Israeli dominance, the failure of peace, and the fragmentation and weakness of the Arab world in the face of the West."[21]

The link between violence and religion is significant. The depiction of political goals in absolute terms provides justification for extreme measures. "For militants [jihad] conveys carte blanche to kill, kidnap, hijack and bomb anyone they see as an infidel, including . . . other Muslims."[22] Although this violence is linked to a transcendent order, it remains, fundamentally, a practical tool in the temporal affairs of men. Hamas bombings and other attacks represent tactical decisions designed to achieve specific goals and are not random.[23] By striking at civilians within Israel, Hamas and Islamic Jihad have sought to derail the peace process by undermining Israeli public support for the peace accords.[24]

Popular Arab support of violent acts has magnified the impact on Israeli public opinion. Editorials that condoned suicide bombings in early 1995 and sympathetic reporting in countries such as Egypt, Jordan, and Syria raised questions in the mind of the Israeli public about whether these nations are sincerely interested in peace.[25] Demonstrations in the occupied territories for "martyred" Palestinians shown on Israeli television reinforced this perception.[26]

Although it is the violent tactics that often define Hamas, much of its popular support derives from the organization's role as a social services provider in Gaza and the West Bank.[27] The Muslim Brotherhood spent much of the 1970s developing a social service network to "resocialize the society according to Islamic standards from the mosques, the universities, and an impressive number of charitable associative movements."[28] Today, Hamas continues "to deliver social services (schools, medical clinics, sports clubs, religious community centers, food and money for orphans and poor families) that the Palestinian National Authority or Israeli administration do not provide."[29]

Islamic ideology is another source of popular support. Hamas's ideology portrays politics as the arena of a larger divine drama in which its members play a central role in carrying out God's will. The organization, which defines its program simply as "Islam,"[30] relies upon religion as a source of legitimacy and power, and is therefore careful to defend its actions in religious terms.[31] As with other activist groups, Hamas interprets Islam as a comprehensive set of beliefs encompassing all realms of human existence, and emphasizes the interconnection between religion, politics, and the larger Islamic world.[32] This emphasis has served to universalize the Palestinian struggle and—coupled with the explicit rejection of both secular nationalism and Zionism—to unify Hamas's membership.

While emphasizing its global Islamic appeal, Hamas has also found it expedient, and necessary, to cultivate nationalist sentiments for its Palestinian constituency. Based on its belief that the Palestinian cause is fundamentally an Islamic cause, Hamas has sought to tap into the nationalist fervor long associated with the PLO.[33] Similarly, the PLO has increasingly interjected appeals to religion into its rhetoric. The result, ironically, has been a demonstrable convergence of ideology and symbolism between the PLO (especially the Fatah wing) and Hamas since 1987; it is argued that the Intifada "produced a growing Islamization of Fatah and a nationalization of Hamas."[34]

Hamas and the PLO

While the stated goal of Hamas is to overthrow Israel and establish an Islamic state,[35] Hamas also seeks to distinguish itself from the PLO. The two groups share a common ambition—statehood—and a common constituency—the Palestinian people. Hamas's active opposition to the peace accords (and the PA) can be seen, consequently, as an effort to define itself as the more radical and, hence, the more authentic voice of Palestinian nationalism. At an Institute conference in 1994, it was argued that "a growing part of the Palestinian people considers that Yasir Arafat's administration [is] no longer able to defend its most elementary rights. Therefore, Hamas continues to combine patriotism and integrity in an inclusive Islamic rhetoric [in an effort to become] the legitimate heir of the nationalism of the PLO."[36]

Tensions between Fatah (the PLO's main faction) and Hamas are not new. Having developed outside the PLO organizational structures, Hamas has long represented a challenge to the PLO's status as the sole representative of the Palestinian people.[37] While the two groups have worked collaboratively at times, their relations have more often been strained.[38] With the signing of the Oslo peace accords, Hamas stepped up its opposition to the PLO (and, consequently, the PA), accusing it of "abandoning the rights of the Palestinians, recognizing the Zionist enemy and giving up the armed struggle for the sake of a frail authority."[39]

Failure of the peace accords would leave the Palestinian people further away from an independent state, and the two societies (Israel and the Palestinians in the occupied territories) even more polarized; however, it is believed that such a turn of events would not be unfavorable to Hamas. First, the increased polarization would open the door to a "renewal of the Arab-Israeli conflict on the new terms of a Jewish-Muslim war of religion."[40] Second, failure of the peace process would discredit Arafat and the PLO, leaving Hamas in a dominant position in Gaza and possibly the West Bank. "What comes after Arafat? What comes after Arafat is division and fragmentation, and what will remain is Hamas."[41]

If the PA is successful in establishing a viable and productive autonomous government, however, its success would likely undermine Hamas support among rank-and-file Palestinians.[42] This position is based on Glenn Robinson's argument that support for Hamas is largely derivative: its standing rises and falls in inverse relation to that of PLO's main faction, Fatah. As the PA fails to deliver on its stated intentions, the popularity of Hamas increases; as the PA succeeds, Hamas support falls away.[43] While Hamas's core support would probably remain stable throughout these fluctuations, the "soft" support among the average person on the street varies. "Some observers contend that the support for the radical Palestinian Islamic groups could drop if and when self-rule successfully is extended throughout the occupied territories and if the Palestinian Authority is able to accelerate economic development in the areas under its control."[44]

THE PEACE PROCESS AND DEMOCRATIZATION

The Declaration of Principles on Palestinian Self-Rule (DOP), signed by Israeli Prime Minister Yitzhak Rabin and PLO Chairman Yasir Arafat on September 13, 1993, significantly redefined the Israeli-Palestinian relationship. Though the declaration was just one step in a larger process, it embodied the two leaders' shared perception that the continuation of the Arab-Israeli conflict did not serve the long-term interest of either the Palestinian or the Israeli people. The key provisions of the DOP included mutual recognition of Israel and the PLO, a

timetable for Israeli withdrawal from the occupied territories, and a commitment to a final settlement of the Palestinian issue set for no later than December
1998. While it left major disputes unresolved, the declaration provided a framework for addressing controversial issues, and, most important, for satisfying
the two most basic needs of the parties involved: Palestinian self-rule and Israeli
security.

A series of agreements implementing the Declaration of Principles culminated in the "Oslo II" agreement, signed on September 24, 1995, and completed
the second stage of implementation. This agreement increased the PA's control
over areas of the West Bank, began redeployment of the Israeli Defense Forces
(IDF), and provided for the establishment of a Palestinian police force and a
Palestinian Council. The third and final stage is supposed to address the most
controversial issues left in the negotiations. These include defining the final
borders between Israel and the Palestinian "entity" (and whether or not it
should be a state), the future status of Jerusalem and of the Jewish settlers on
the West Bank, and control of the water resources in the area. This last phase
of negotiations is known as the "Final Status" negotiations, and was originally
set to begin in May 1996.

One criticism made of the Oslo accords is that—unlike the South African preliminary agreement—there was no initial agreement on the ultimate goal of the
negotiations.[45] The most difficult issues were left unresolved, with the agreement that they would be addressed in the later stages of negotiation. While no
agreement would have been reached without these stipulations, the failure to
agree initially on the establishment of a Palestinian state left many
Palestinians—and not just Islamist activists—disgruntled. As a result, many have
viewed the Declaration of Principles as a capitulation to Israel.[46] Many Israelis,
on the other hand, feel the subsequent agreements implementing the accord
give far too much to the Palestinians for little, if anything, in return.

It is difficult at this point for members of either side to appreciate the advantages of the peace process. Improvements in the Israeli economy and the
country's diplomatic relations have been overshadowed by concern among the
Israeli public that its "daily exposure to the danger of terrorism has increased."[47]
Similarly, Jewish settlers see the process as infringing upon their rights. For their
part, Palestinians also have been subject to violence, such as the killing of
Muslim worshipers in Hebron by American-born Baruch Goldstein, while Jewish
settlement in the West Bank reinforces images of Israeli domination. Many
Palestinians have also not felt themselves to be real partners in the peace

process, nor have they gained much from it in practical terms. As one U.S. official commented in Senate testimony, "The peace dividend expected by many Palestinians has not yet been reflected in economic conditions in [Gaza] and the West Bank. Slow foreign investment, border closures and high unemployment and underemployment have exacerbated popular frustration with the slow pace of negotiations."[48]

The major obstacles to the peace process, then, include political violence (particularly that of Islamic activists) and the absence of tangible benefits. The difficulty of dealing with these issues has hindered the implementation of the agreements already reached, and has also undermined support for further concessions. The PA's perceived ineffectiveness or unwillingness to deal with militant violence through much of 1995 limited support among Israelis for withdrawing the IDF from the occupied territories. Conversely, continued Jewish settlement (resumed under the government of Prime Minister Benjamin Netanyahu), the indeterminacy of the peace process, and the closure of the borders between Israel and the occupied territories have all limited Palestinian enthusiasm for the peace process.

The continued opposition and violence of the more extreme opponents to the agreement, particularly Hamas, have evoked responses from both Israel and the PA that have raised concerns among human rights advocates. The use of harsh interrogation methods by Israeli authorities, justified by the "necessity defense," has elicited criticism from human rights organizations and activists.[49] Similarly, the PA's use of emergency military courts and other repressive means to constrain dissent has been a subject of criticism. The PA's reliance upon the PLO security services betrays the absence of enduring civil and legal structures in the emerging polity[50] and brings into question the nature of the developing Palestinian "entity."[51]

U.S. POLICY

Measures to restrain activist opposition to the peace process are argued to be unavoidable—in the short run—if regimes such as Jordan or the PA are to normalize relations with Israel.[52] However, autocratic rule in the region is not perceived as conducive to long-term stability and is not in keeping with stated U.S. policy. The task for U.S. policymakers, then, is to reconcile these apparently conflicting objectives of pursuing a peace settlement and democratization, while also maintaining regional stability.

The inherent tension between political liberalization, the containment of Islamism, and the participation in a negotiated settlement with Israel, [coupled with] the reality of relatively weak states, will restrict [Arab] regimes to the pursuit of at most two of these policy goals. [Consequently], the movement toward democratization will be stunted. That is, contrary to many optimistic forecasts . . . the end of the Arab-Israeli conflict will likely usher in a new era of authoritarianism.[53]

Jordan

Jordan's efforts to reach out to its Islamic opposition and to institutionalize Islam within the governing process have been effective in mitigating extremism in the past. As a result, the country has been able to avoid the violence that has plagued other nations in the region. However, the increased radicalization of the Islamic opposition and its vocal opposition to the peace process threaten this policy of inclusion. The rejectionist message of the Islamic activists has popular appeal. "Islamic groups have been the prime beneficiaries of the anger and frustration of even highly educated Jordanians, whose expectations of rising social and economic status are left unfulfilled in [a] climate of austerity, recession, and mass unemployment."[54]

The significance of Jordan's economic and political problems were demonstrated by antigovernment riots that erupted in August 1996 after an increase in the price of bread. The price hikes followed a reduction in the government subsidy, a reduction prompted by International Monetary Fund requirements for extending further credits to the country. While the riots were triggered by economic issues, they had broader implications. "Though bread was the immediate impetus, most [Jordanians] . . . agreed that the price hikes had touched deep frustrations among Jordan's poor over the lack of any tangible dividends from recent developments—the introduction of limited democracy, the IMF program and, above all, the peace with Israel signed in 1994."[55]

U.S. policy toward Jordan has been to encourage and support King Hussein's reconciliation efforts by providing security assurances, along with financial and economic assistance. In his speech to the Jordanian Parliament, President Clinton outlined a series of measures that his administration has adopted to help address the challenges faced by the Jordanian regime. These include the following:

▶ forgiving Jordan's existing debt to the United States;

▶ establishing a U.S.-Jordan-Israel Trilateral Economic Commission;

▶ creating a Middle East Bank for Cooperation and Development;

▶ establishing a $75 million investment fund by the Overseas Private Investment Corporation to encourage U.S. investment in the region; and

▶ supporting efforts to expand trade and investment opportunities, which will include a bilateral investment treaty and a lowering of existing trade barriers.

These efforts, which have been largely implemented, are aimed at providing "tangible results" for Jordan's participation in, and support of, the peace process. "Those who take the risks for peace must not stand alone," declared President Clinton. "We will work with Jordan to meet your legitimate defense requirements, and to give you the security you deserve. But for peace to endure, it must not only provide protection, it must produce tangible improvements in the quality of ordinary citizens' lives, and in so doing, give those citizens a real stake in preserving the peace."[56]

West Bank and Gaza

Actively pursuing peace in the Middle East is a top priority of U.S. policy. A viable Arab-Israeli peace agreement is perceived as the key to stabilizing the region and an effective means of "placing extremists on the defensive and increas[ing] their isolation."[57] Implementation of the DOP, however, has not been easy. Political violence perpetrated by Hamas and Islamic Jihad—including a series of bombings in Israel in 1995 and 1996—had a strong effect on Israeli public opinion, and brought into question the ability of the peace process to provide security for Israel and its citizens. Similarly, continued Jewish settlement in the West Bank, poor economic conditions, and the early reluctance of Prime Minister Benjamin Netanyahu to implement key parts of the existing peace agreement generated deep discontent among Palestinians. This discontent erupted into violence when the Netanyahu government opened an archaeological tunnel in Jerusalem near several Muslim holy sites. The violence was the worst in the area since the Oslo agreement was reached in 1993, and was marked by gun battles between Israeli troops and Palestinian police.

Palestinians and many observers have attributed the September 1996 violence to Israeli provocations. News reports, however, also indicate that groups such as Hamas not only were active in the protests but also encouraged protesters to attack Israeli checkpoints. The ability of Palestinian leader Yasir Arafat to constrain the violence was limited by both of these factors. Forcefully suppressing the protests (and Hamas) would have undermined Arafat's legitimacy since public opinion among Palestinians strongly supported the protests. At the same time, the Netanyahu government's actions and policies since coming to power did little to encourage Palestinian support for the peace process. "Arafat is in a Catch-22. Israelis place on him the responsibility to stop violence, while at the same time refusing concessions that might strengthen his political standing. If goaded Palestinian police fire on Israeli troops, Arafat is held responsible. If he claims he's not in full control, he gives Israeli hard-liners a reason to refuse to negotiate."[58]

The underlying issue here is not new, and was raised at the Institute meeting in December 1994. At that time, the debate was over whether or not U.S. policymakers should pressure the PA to crack down on Hamas and Islamic Jihad. At the Institute meeting, Glenn Robinson warned that such a step could "lead to the disintegration of the peace process,"[59] since it could undermine the already fragile position of the PA. This point was supported by those who feared continued alienation of the Palestinian community. Martin Kramer, however, argued for a forceful response to the militants, noting that no governing body can rule with a hostile, armed group in its midst. Kramer further argued that the continuing violence undermines the ability of the Israeli government to make concessions; therefore, Arafat will ultimately have no choice but "to suppress the armed elements."[60]

The differences in these two approaches reflected the essential disagreement among the roundtable participants over both the nature of Islamic activism as a whole and how policymakers should respond. The first approach perceived Islamic activism as primarily a social movement and argued for a policy of limited inclusion. Distinguishing between moderates and extremists, this approach sought to "co-opt" the large grassroots following and isolate the militants. It was argued that the most viable means of containing militant action lies in the success of the peace accords to provide tangible benefits to the Palestinian people. Making peace work will provide an incentive for those within Hamas who would be willing to work with the PA, while collapse of the accords will strengthen those who advocate continued confrontation. "There is an inverse relationship between the strength of Hamas and real breakthroughs on the ground; a good settlement is the surest way to weaken Hamas and deradicalize most of what remains."[61]

The second approach opposed any accommodation with Hamas.[62] The organization's willingness to use violence against civilians, it was argued, raises serious questions about the desirability of bringing it into the political process.

The best course of action, according to this line of thinking, is to pressure the PA to crack down on Hamas and Islamic Jihad, and to hold the PA responsible for the terrorist activities of these groups. For its part, the U.S. government should restrict the funding that Hamas receives from the United States—estimated at close to a third of Hamas's income—even if that means closing the organization's charitable fronts.[63] Finally, this approach advocated keeping Hamas on the Anti-Terrorist List and refusing any direct contacts between the U.S. State Department and Hamas.

These two approaches reflect the debate within Hamas itself over whether it is primarily a social movement or a militant, political organization. The outcome of this debate will determine whether Hamas, as an organization, is able and willing to operate within the emerging political system and will indicate the extent to which it is "co-optable."

While the two approaches appear to be antithetical, there was some common ground on specific issues. For example, both sides agreed that a peace agreement is in the long-term interests of all concerned, and that the real threat to the process is political violence—by either side. Furthermore, both groups agreed that eradicating violence depends on continued progress in the peace process, and, ultimately, on reaching a final agreement that provides the benefits that give Palestinians a stake in the system. Both approaches also recognized that—even if the peace process does succeed—there exists a core group of militants who will probably never work within the system, since their interests are so clearly opposed to those of the PA.

Finally, on the central policy question of pressuring the PA to crack down on Hamas, both sides did agree that if done in conjunction with real concessions by Israel, efforts by the PA to control militant activity would not undermine the fledgling Palestinian authority. To this end, there needs to be a concerted effort to fully implement the terms of the DOP before a PA crackdown. Martin Kramer argued that within this context, Israel cannot renege on its commitment to redeploy IDF forces, and "must stay the course" on the issue of Jewish settlements and continued occupation. Glenn Robinson agreed, although he argued that this next step forward should also include a statement of principles that "makes explicit what is implicit, that at the end of the day there will be two states."[64] Only then, after providing the two-state solution and demonstrating greater commitment to the peace process, "will the PA be in a position (as it is not now) to crack down on the fringe elements of Hamas."[65]

UPDATE

Since the December 1994 working group meeting, a number of significant events have occurred. Despite a series of bombings through 1995—and a related decline in Israeli public support for the peace process—a series of agreements implementing the DOP were reached. As previously mentioned, these included the Oslo II agreement, which marked the culmination of the second stage of implementation. Among other things, this agreement established an eighty-two-seat Palestinian Council, elections for which were held in the West Bank and Gaza on January 20, 1996. Although Hamas officially boycotted the elections, individual supporters of Hamas did run and were elected.

While the second-stage agreement was greeted with criticism from both Israelis and Palestinians, the withdrawal of Israeli troops from the major urban centers on the West Bank and the subsequent elections provided Palestinians with a greater sense of progress, and temporarily blunted the appeal of Hamas's rejectionist posture. It was reported at that time that Hamas, in fear of being overtaken by events, was divided between those who would seek dialogue with the PA and those who continued to advocate militant opposition to the peace process.[66] According to certain observers, Hamas leaders "fear[ed] irrelevance more than compromise."[67]

In November 1995, Prime Minister Yitzhak Rabin was assassinated by a young Jewish extremist. Although the loss of Rabin was seen as a significant blow to the peace process, Israeli public support for the process—particularly the Oslo II agreement—increased in the aftermath of the shooting. Rabin's successor, Shimon Peres, continued implementation of the second-stage agreement, and pledged to push forward with the third, and final, stage of the negotiations. Rabin's funeral also marked a new level of Israeli acceptance by its Arab neighbors; seven Arab states and the PA were represented at the event.

Israeli elections in May 1996 resulted in the coming to power of a new government. Likud leader Benjamin Netanyahu was elected prime minister in Israel's first direct election for that post, and formed a governing coalition even though Peres's Labor Party had won a plurality of seats in the Israeli parliament.[68] The Likud victory was due in part to the fallout from a series of suicide bombings that took place in the weeks preceding the elections. The bombings, carried out by Hamas militants, eroded public support for then–Prime Minister Peres and thrust the issue of security to the forefront of the campaign. While the final results did not indicate opposition to the peace process per se, they did reflect Israeli concern about personal security and the way in which the peace process was taking shape. As one newly elected official noted, "Ironically, the Arabs, through Hamas and the perceived threat to the personal security of the Israelis it posed, ended up determining who will be Israel's prime minister."[69]

The election of Netanyahu raised many questions about the future of the peace process, particularly after the new government reestablished a proactive settlement policy and after Palestinian protests in September 1996 turned violent. In January 1997, however, an agreement was reached between Netanyahu and Arafat that provided for further Israeli troop withdrawals and a reaffirmation of commitments made under previous agreements. This agreement, known as the Hebron Agreement, was significant because it was the first agreement reached between the new prime minister and the PA. Many analysts saw it as a victory of pragmatism over ideology; though neither side had relinquished their fundamental concerns, the accord's broad support reflected a significant constituency for peace. It was also seen as strengthening the PA vis-à-vis Hamas. "Just as Mr. Arafat has plainly gained the upper hand against Hamas in Gaza and in other West Bank cities, many Palestinians say the release of Hebron from Israel's grasp is likely to add to the Palestinian leader's authority."[70]

Subsequent events, however, have brought the peace process to a standstill. The Israeli government's support for new settlements on disputed territory in East Jerusalem and a suicide bombing in Tel Aviv in March 1997 sparked a renewed cycle of violence and daily street confrontations between Israeli soldiers and Palestinian activists. These events reinforced a historical perception of bad faith on both sides and undermined what little trust existed between the two communities. The Palestinian Authority complained that the new settlements were an effort by Israel to resolve a disputed issue outside the negotiation process, while the Israeli government charged Arafat with giving a "green light" to Hamas for the Tel Aviv bombing.

Negotiations between the Netanyahu government and the PA consequently deadlocked and public support in both communities for a negotiated solution has waned. Israeli support for the peace process has once again been shaken by political violence, while Palestinians have been outraged by new settlements. The shift in attitudes on both sides is reflected in a poll conducted by the Nablus-based Center for Palestine Research and Studies. The poll found that a majority of Palestinians believed that "there is no possibility [of] reach[ing] a solution acceptable to the two parties," and that 38 percent of those polled (double the previous year's result) felt that a return to "armed attacks" was warranted.[71]

Public opinion polls in Israel indicate a similar pessimism over the viability of peace with the Palestinians and Israel's Arab neighbors. While the peace process may not be dead, it certainly has experienced a setback.

4

PAKISTAN AND
SOUTH ASIA

Islamic activism in Pakistan has been dominated historically by the Jama'at-i-Islami, an Islamic organization established by Mawlana Mawdudi in 1941, six years before the partition of British-ruled India. The Jama'at has been an effective pressure group in mainstream Pakistani politics and has worked closely with several incumbent regimes. Although frequently in the opposition, it has been far less militant and antistatist than similar groups elsewhere, relying instead upon constitutional and legal means for achieving its goals. As one commentator has noted, "While Mawdudi's ideas are revolutionary, his methods are evolutionary."[1]

The inclusion of the Jama'at in the political process has mitigated its ideological demands and shaped its largely accommodationist methods. Although never able to secure power in its own right, it has been extremely influential through its grassroots activism. The so-called street power of the Jama'at has helped it to frame public debate on such key national dialogues as the development of the 1956 and the 1973 constitutions. The Jama'at has also provided political support and religious legitimacy to ruling parties when such actions served the Jama'at's interests.

The impact of the Jama'at-i-Islami, however, is not limited to South Asia. The Jama'at has been an organizational model for other Islamic groups, and Mawdudi is regarded as "one of the chief ideologists of Islamic revivalism in the modern period."[2] Mawdudi provided activist movements with a systematic formulation of Islamic policies. His conceptions of "Islamic ideology," "Islamic economics," "Islamic revolution," and "reconstruction of the Prophetic community" remain "closely associated with political Islam today."[3]

The predominance of the Jama'at in Pakistan, however, is diminishing. The rise of ethnic and sectarian parties and the flourishing of a "Kalashnikov culture" in the post–Afghan war period have strengthened militants at the expense of more mainstream activists. The militants—many linked to the thriving drug trade—seriously undermine the stability of Pakistan and threaten the social fabric of the region. A group of army officers linked to one such sectarian party was arrested in October 1995 for allegedly plotting to overthrow the Bhutto regime in order to "turn Pakistan into a fundamentalist state."[4]

The history of the Jama'at-i-Islami—along with the recent rise of sectarian parties—tells us much about the evolution of Islamic activism in South Asia. The division of the Jama'at at partition and the separate development of splinter groups in Bangladesh, India, and Kashmir provide a glimpse into the differing manifestations of the movement. The characteristics of the various groups reflect their diverse backgrounds and, significantly, the different political exigencies each has faced. Marginalization in India, inclusion in Pakistan, and violent conflict in Kashmir have shaped the means and ends that each group has pursued. In his presentation to the Institute working group, Vali Nasr of the University of San Diego noted that while the newer sectarian parties vividly illustrate the dangers of Islamic militancy to civil society, "the case of South Asia [as a whole] has presaged the participation of Islamic movements in the democratic process and can tell us much about what to expect from political Islam in more open political climates across the Muslim world."[5]

JAMA'AT-I-ISLAMI IN PAKISTAN

Born in British-ruled India at the beginning of the twentieth century, Mawlana Mawdudi wrote extensively on Islam under European colonial rule. Influenced by the two world wars, the dismemberment of the Ottoman Empire, and the establishment of Israel, Mawdudi's writings reflected the intellectual, spiritual, and political crisis precipitated by foreign domination. The general response by the Muslim community in India to the challenge of the West had been split between those who wished to withdraw from it and those who sought to embrace it. Mawdudi, however, represented a third approach—that of challenging the West with a "self-assertive Islamic nationalism."[6]

Like Sayyid Qutb in Egypt, Mawdudi drew upon the eighteenth- and nineteenth-century Islamic reformers, appropriating their worldview and their emphasis on political action.[7] Placing the blame for India's social ills at the feet of European imperialism and a Westernized Muslim elite, he argued for a return to Islamic principles and for a rejection of Western secularism. This message resonated with many who perceived Western culture as a threat to the very identity of the Muslim peoples. In this way, Mawdudi and the Jama'at "appeared to be the defenders of Islam against the inroads of foreign political and intellectual domination."[8]

The Jama'at's ideology emphasized (1) the establishment of an Islamic constitution and the use of the *shari'a* as a blueprint for society; (2) God as the basis of sovereignty;[9] (3) the Qur'an and Sunna as the foundation for interpreting Islam; (4) a strong belief that a principled society will be rewarded with material success; and, above all, (5) the all-encompassing nature of Islam for "individual and corporate life, state and society."[10]

> [An Islamic state's] sphere of activity is coextensive with the whole of human life.
> . . . In such a state no one can regard any field of his affairs as personal and private. Considered from this aspect the Islamic state bears a kind of resemblance to the Fascist and Communist states. But you will find later on that, despite its all-inclusiveness, it is something vastly and basically different from the modern totalitarian and authoritarian states. Individual liberty is not suppressed under it nor is there any trace of dictatorship in it.[11]

The Jama'at's emphasis on integrating Islam into political affairs was based upon a belief that Pakistan's social ills were rooted in the unbelief of the existing rulers and in previous efforts to separate religion from politics. Secular ideologies—which included both Marxism and capitalism—were thought to embody materialist values that corrupt society. The restoration of past glories depended, then, on returning an errant community to its traditional emphasis upon revealed truth. This meant, in practice, "the total subordination of the institutions of civil society and the state to the authority of divine law as revealed in the Qur'an and practiced by the Prophet."[12]

A final defining characteristic of the Jama'at has been its emphasis on political action as a means for religious and social reform. The Jama'at's early efforts focused on developing a small core group of believers that would provide the basis for the organization and work to acquire political power. It eventually became "one of the best organized, disciplined, religio-political organizations of South Asia, [and] served as a model for many Islamic political movements in the Muslim world."[13] It effectively used modern technologies and mass communications to get its message out, and—though originally opposed to the creation of Pakistan and the leadership of Muhammad Ali Jinnah—became a leading voice in the political process of the newly founded Islamic Republic of Pakistan.

68

The Jama'at's Role in Key Events

The Jama'at opposed the secular tendencies of the early leaders of Pakistan, and mobilized its supporters to influence the first major political debate of the newly established state: the drafting of a constitution. During the constitutional debate, "Jama'at emerged as the sole spokesman for Islam and the Islamic state."[14] Its effectiveness in shaping public debate was partly the result of the Jama'at's disciplined organization and focus, and partly the result of the weakness and disorganization of all other parties. The passage of the Objectives Resolution in 1949, a preliminary declaration of principles committing the state to some form of Islamic framework, was an early victory for the Jama'at.

Even so, the constitution ultimately adopted in 1956 fell far short of what the Islamic activists had sought. To the contrary, it contained a Western legal framework modeled on British parliamentary democracy. However, even though it did not significantly alter the status quo, the constitution did contain enough references to the Qur'an and Sunna to appease Mawdudi and his supporters.

> The content of the constitution and the kind of state it aimed to create were strongly tilted in the direction of the modernist preferences. In accepting it, Mawdudi not only seemed to deny much of what he had previously insisted upon as characteristic of an Islamic state but, indeed, left intact very little that would distinguish him form the liberal constitutionalists he had previously so bitterly criticized for their un-Islamic ways.[15]

The Jama'at-i-Islami opposed the military rule of the late 1950s and early 1960s, although direct confrontation with the regime was limited to such issues as family law reform. The Jama'at had hoped to strengthen its position by participating in elections that were originally scheduled for 1959, but were later canceled by the regime. Despite the official ban on political parties, the Jama'at remained a viable force by maintaining its network of operatives as a religious organization. A 1964 government crackdown on the Jama'at followed a period of intensified and outspoken protest. The regime's actions, however, were reversed by a Supreme Court decision voiding the government's ban on the organization. The rise of socialism and ethnic tensions forced the Jama'at-i-Islami to reevaluate long-held positions on social reform, resulting in greater support for the status quo. Zulifikar Bhutto's socialist alternative threatened the role of Islam as a central ordering principle of society, and fundamentally changed the nature of debate about the future of Pakistan. The increased emphasis on economic issues relegated religious matters to a secondary position. The separatist movement in East Pakistan (Bangladesh) similarly undermined the primacy of Islamic reform. "The alarming prospects of the rise of secular, socialist, and regionalist political forces had in fact left the Jama'at with no option but to support the existing power structures, which at least paid lip service to Islam."[16]

The Jama'at-i-Islami participated with government forces in military action against the Bengali separatists in East Pakistan, and worked with business interests, right-wing organizations, and others in opposition to the socialist movement. This latter effort was also marked by violence. This period "witnessed the transformation of the Jama'at's students' wing, the Islami Jam'iyat-i-Tulaba (IJT), from a peaceful da'wah organization into a militant force, willing to meet violence with violence."[17]

Amid this turmoil, elections were held in 1970. The Jama'at-i-Islami participated, but fared extremely poorly, winning only four seats in a National Assembly of three hundred representatives. Ironically, the elected assembly—dominated by the socialist Pakistan People's Party—adopted a constitution in 1973 that retained the Islamic provisions of the 1956 constitution and made Islam the state religion.[18] While the content of the constitution is a testament to the power of religious appeals within the political system, it is also the result of skilled Jama'at parliamentarians and the Jama'at's ability to mobilize support and manipulate the system to its own ends. This ability to shape public debate also characterized the 1977 elections, where Islamic issues were politicized to such an extent that the socialist prime minister, Zulifikar Bhutto, was forced to put forward Islamic reforms in the postelection period. "Since the mid-1970s, the Jama'at's street power has been an important element in national politics, as a means of creating unrest against governments."[19]

When the Bhutto regime was overthrown by General Zia-ul-Haq in 1977, the new military regime invited the Jama'at to participate in the government. The party readily accepted, assuming that Zia would fulfill his commitment to carry out his stated program of Islamization. However, in 1979, the four Jama'at Cabinet ministers resigned their posts—after a period of ineffectiveness—over the indefinite postponement of general elections. For several years Jama'at remained in "uneasy coexistence" with the Zia regime, opposing the absence of democracy but finding common ground on other issues, including the burgeoning war in Afghanistan.

Inclusion vs. Exclusion

The ability of the Jama'at-i-Islami to influence the political process in Pakistan provided it with a stake in the system and tempered the organization's revolutionary zeal. Unlike other Islamic movements, the Jama'at did not evolve into an antistate organization reliant upon covert and violent activities.[20] Rather, it developed in direct response to the imperatives of open political activity, and consistently sought gains through the electoral system. As Mawdudi commented after the passage of the Objectives Resolution in 1949, "Now that this has become a regularized Islamic state, it is no longer the country of the enemy against which it is our duty to strive. Rather, it is now the country of friends, our own country, the strengthening, construction, and progress of which are our duty."[21]

The role that Jama'at sought to play within the system was that of religious arbiter, which it fulfilled by conferring religious legitimacy upon the state; "by mobilizing Islamic symbols and its traditional spokesmen, the 'ulama,' the [Jama'at] has made religion available to the state for political ends."[22] Since Pakistan was originally conceived as an Islamic state, it was Islam that provided a unifying identity to those who left India at partition.[23] Furthermore, appeals to religion were recognized by political leaders early on as a means of diverting attention from pressing, even intractable problems.[24]

While there have been efforts to constrain the activities of the Jama'at and imprison its leaders, the various Pakistani regimes were never as successful or as brutal in suppressing Islamic activist opposition as were regimes in Egypt, Iran, and elsewhere. The absence of extremely repressive policies is linked to the weakness of the Pakistani regimes and the inherent popularity of Islam among the Pakistani people. The existence of an independent judiciary also provided political parties with the opportunity to work within the system. As a result, the Jama'at worked within the mainstream of Pakistani politics and did not develop extremist tendencies. "One can argue that it is usually the repressive policies of governments and the total absence of freedom to pursue normal political activities that tend to drive religious and other political groups to radicalism and violent methods of change."[25]

While the Objectives Resolution exemplifies the ability of the Jama'at to shape the frame of debate in Pakistan, it also demonstrates the Jama'at's willingness to compromise on significant ideological issues. As noted above, the organization's acceptance of the resolution's secular legal structure was surprising, the Islamic references notwithstanding. Similarly, the Jama'at's support for the ruling military regime against the Bengali separatists highlighted the in-congruities between the organization's professed democratic ideology and its practice. Jama'at's support for the Zia regime further demonstrated the mod-erating—some would say corrupting—influence of political participation. "It is really quite incredible the degree to which Jama'at-i-Islami has not only become part of the system, but has been co-opted and used by various regimes."[26]

Although the ideological compromises and pragmatism demanded by polit-ical participation worked against the development of zealous extremism, the Jama'at's emphasis on worldly success at the expense of ideology led some members to complain that it was too much of a political party and not enough of a revivalist movement.[27] The political process further diminished the Jama'at's influence by allowing other Islamic parties to compete for the same constituency and by giving the state and secular groups the opportunity to out-maneuver the Islamic opposition.[28]

For these reasons, the Jama'at's ability to mobilize its followers and influ-ence the political process never translated into electoral success. Between 1970 and 1988, four national elections were held in Pakistan. In none of these did the Jama'at-i-Islami gain more than ten seats in the National Assembly. The com-petition and rivalry with other Islamic parties for religious votes was particu-larly significant: "[The two traditional *ulama* parties] have in fact challenged the Islamic religious credentials of the Jama'at more vehemently than the sec-ular parties."[29] The poor electoral showing of the Jama'at also reflects the ur-ban base of the organization in a country where 70 percent of the population lives in rural areas. Finally, the religious divisions between Shi'ite and Sunni populations also figure into this equation; the Shi'ites—who make up anywhere from 10 to 25 percent of the population—tend to support secular parties.

While it can be argued that the Jama'at has been tempered by the moderat-ing influence of political involvement, it can also be argued that the Pakistani political process has been similarly influenced by the Jama'at's agenda. The in-clusion process has entailed compromises by the Pakistani state as well as by the Jama'at, and has led to the passage of controversial "Islamic" laws. The Zia regime, in particular, proved "very willing to sacrifice minority rights"[30] to ap-pease the Jama'at and keep it away from more central sociopolitical and eco-nomic policies. The "cost" of such compromises upon society is impossible to determine, but it is argued that the legacy has adversely affected Pakistani so-ciety. "The government [of Benazir Bhutto]," noted a participant in the Institute discussion, "seems to be hamstrung by the fact that it has let the Jama'at be its vehicle for understanding religion in the polity as a whole, rather than looking at what is going on at the grassroots level."[31]

INDIA

According to one working group participant, "fundamentalist Islam is not a major force in India. The real source of concern in India is the rise of religiously based majoritarianism in the form of militant Hindu political parties and their allies."[32] Many of the Muslim activists in India left for Pakistan at partition in 1947. The people and the organizations that remained, like the Jama'at-i-Islami of India, focused on education, social welfare projects, and spiritual teaching, largely opting not to participate in the political process. Furthermore, the dominance of the secular Congress party in India, coupled with the minority status of the Muslim community, precluded Islamic activism from realistically asserting such goals as the establishment of an Islamic state. Instead, the Islamic movements in India focused on maintaining their identity and language within a predominantly Hindu society. The marginalization of the Jama'at and similar groups forced them to become "essentially a missionary movement dedicated to the long-run goal of promoting Islam among both Muslims and Hindus."[33]

The role of the Indian Jama'at as representative of a minority group is telling. It has worked with other Muslim groups within the Indian political process to mitigate the effects of Hindu communalism. In the 1960s the Jama'at joined a coalition of Muslim political parties to promote "national unity and harmony on the basis of shared religious values and within the parameters of a multiracial, multilingual, and multicultural Indian society."[34] The thrust of this effort was to safeguard its distinct religion, identity, and language within a larger country. By contrast, the Jama'at in Pakistan was involved in the Anti-Ahmadhiya movement, which has been characterized as an "antiminority pogrom."[35] Similarly, in Bangladesh, Islamic activism has been associated with the suppression of religious rights of the minority Jumma peoples, a collection of Buddhist groups in the Chittagong Hill tracts. Whereas the Jama'at in India has been a staunch advocate of secularism, the Jama'at in Pakistan denounces secularism as "an evil force."[36]

BANGLADESH

As mentioned above, the Jama'at-i-Islami opposed Bangladeshi separatism and openly collaborated with the central Pakistani government in the 1971 civil war, supplying arms and men to fight the separatist movement. The paramilitary group, formed predominantly by Jama'at's student wing, fought side by side with the Pakistani army. The group's opposition to an independent Bangladesh was based on the belief in the universality of Islam; a separate state would represent a failure for the unifying capacity of Islamic nationalism. Because of its role in the civil war, the Jama'at was banned from the newly established country of Bangladesh. Many of the group's leaders fled to Pakistan, and many of its members were killed or imprisoned in Bangladesh.

Despite its opposition to the Bangladeshi independence, the Jama'at has emerged as a strong and popular movement in postindependence Bangladesh. The organization reestablished itself to oppose the secular nationalism of the ruling socialist regime, the Awami League. By maintaining a low profile and focusing on education, the organization was able to rebuild itself during the late 1970s. The Jama'at returned as a significant force with the military overthrow of the Awami League. "By the mid-1980's the Awami League was exhausted, socialism was discredited, and the military government of General Husain Ershad was looking to Islam to bolster its rule."[37]

The Jama'at fared well in the elections of 1990–91, winning eighteen seats and 6 percent of the national vote. It subsequently joined the ruling coalition of Prime Minister Khalda Zia. Participation in the government has not been without its costs, however. The Awami League has continued to attack the Jama'at representatives, pointing out their roles in the 1970 civil war in order to discredit them. However, the strong Islamic support in Bangladesh has minimized the effect of these attacks. Furthermore, the Islamic legitimacy that Jama'at confers has helped to bolster the existing government over the last few years.[38]

KASHMIR

During the first few decades of its existence, the Kashmiri Jama'at focused on its religious message, opting not to participate actively in the region's politics. Secular Muslim nationalists dominated the political arena in Kashmir, and the

Jama'at was relegated to the role of a purely religious organization. This changed with the Iranian revolution and with the collapse of relations between Srinigar and Delhi during Rajiv Gandhi's rule. The Kashmiri Jama'at sought to Islamize the conflict in an effort to substitute its own creed for secular nationalism as the guiding ideology for Kashmiri national aspirations.

The effectiveness of the Jama'at's message in Kashmir is due in large measure to the success of the Islamic movements in Iran and Afghanistan. The Pakistani government deliberately attempted to use "Islamic militancy against the Indians in a similar manner to what [was] done against the Soviets."[39] Many of the Jama'at's members were trained in Afghanistan during the war with the Soviet Union. The Jama'at also brought in tactics and rhetoric from the Afghanistan campaign, carrying over to Kashmir the mixture of politics, Islam, and violence that worked so well in the Afghanistan jihad.

Although the Jama'at's *mujahidin* emerged as a well-armed and well-funded organization, it has not been able to command the kind of popular support enjoyed by other groups, such as the Jammu Kashmir Liberation Front. This is due in part to the Kashmiri Jama'at's advocacy of unification with Pakistan, a position that does not enjoy widespread support among Kashmiris.[40] In an effort to undermine support for all the various militant groups, the Indian government held elections in Kashmir in September 1996. Though disputed, the elections brought to power a pro-Indian state government led by a Muslim Kashmiri named Farooq Abdullah. Whether the new government can end the fighting in Kashmir, however, remains to be seen. A significant number of militants continue to operate in Kashmir, and many of the underlying grievances that gave rise to the situation remain. Some analysts argue that the root of the problem is not Islam or Pakistan, but the "denial of democracy and [the] abuse of human rights"[41] in the region.

THE RISE OF SECTARIAN PARTIES IN PAKISTAN AND AFGHANISTAN

The growing sectarian and ethnic rivalries throughout South Asia today are "the most dangerous and significant development[s] in South Asian political Islam."[42] Mainstream movements are being sidelined by the rise of militant religious groups less devoted to ideology and process than to the "Kalashnikov culture." Pakistan has become a haven for such groups in the aftermath of the Afghan war. The government appears to be either unable or unwilling to control the groups, which are often funded by outside sources. "[Militants] have continued to thrive [in Pakistan] and Afghanistan because of the easy availability of cheap and sophisticated weapons—many of which can be traced to the more than $1 billion per year that the United States gave to Afghan militias based in Pakistan during the war against the Soviets."[43]

The violence of the sectarian parties threatens to fracture Pakistani society along religious and ethnic lines. The sectarians seek not only to Islamize society and politics, but to do so by eliminating other religious communities and minorities, most notably the Shi'ites.[44] Iranian efforts in the early 1980s to organize Shi'ites in Pakistan created tensions with the Sunni community, alarming both the Saudi Arabian and the Iraqi governments. The Iraqis and Saudis subsequently sought to offset Iranian influence in Pakistan by funding anti-Shi'ite coalitions. "An [anti-Shi'ite] alliance emerged between Wahhabi [elements], . . . the Muslim Brotherhood, the Jama'at, and the . . . 'ulama.' The result was that the Iran-Iraq war was transplanted into Pakistan with catastrophic effects for the civil order in the country."[45]

In recent years, the Jama'at-i-Islami—concerned "with the fracturing of the polity"[46]—has distanced itself from the anti-Shi'ite coalition. The Saudi and Iraqi funders, however, have continued to use the sectarian parties to oppose Shi'ite activity, giving rise to formal anti-Shi'ite political parties, most notably the Sepah-i-Sahabah Party (Army of the Prophet's Companions, SSP) and the Sunni Tahrik (Sunni Movement). The recruits of these parties come from the seminaries established during the Zia period. The seminary graduates "are religiously inclined but are not thoroughly steeped in religious learning. They were led to expect much from the Islamicization of Pakistan but now have difficulty finding employment. Moreover, given the involvement of the religious establishment in the Afghan war, the use of weapons and violence are easily justifiable for them."[47]

The rise of the new parties also has international implications. These groups are reportedly responsible for training militants fighting in Kashmir,[48] Bosnia, Tajikistan, and the Philippines. "Since the end of the Afghan war in 1989, Pakistani officials estimate that at least ten thousand Islamic militants have been trained by various groups in the Pakistan-Afghanistan border areas."[49] The governments in Egypt, Algeria, and Jordan have also complained that Pakistani militants have been involved in the extremist movements in their countries.

These are some of the unintended consequences of the Afghan war. While the Afghan resistance was critical in defeating the Soviets (and hastening the end of the Cold War), it also spawned a well-armed activist network.[50] The

Jama'at-i-Islami was "an integral part in the effort in getting the Soviets out of Afghanistan,"[51] and it subsequently placed the Islamist ideology at the center of an international network of activists. The men who came from around the world to fight in the Afghan jihad took a knowledge of tactics and ideology back to their homelands. Once the war was over, the "movement [began] looking for a cause, [and] the militants . . . for something to do."[52]

U.S. POLICY

The differences among Islamic groups throughout South Asia provide insight into the nature of Islamic activism and the implications for U.S. foreign policy. The example of Pakistan illustrates how political inclusion can provide incentives for moderation. While the Jama'at worked actively in the political process to further its agenda, the political process "conceded only as much as it need[ed] to keep Islamists under control."[53] In India and Kashmir, the differing status of the various Islamic activists determined very different modes of operation as well as starkly divergent interpretations of Islamic ideology.

The existing situation, however, is complicated by the rise of various militant ethno-religious groups that are at odds with one another and with a weak central government. Large-scale heroin trafficking and a thriving arms trade have also emerged as powerful forces in the aftermath of the Afghan war. The overall situation is marked by unrest and a potential for violence. Government efforts to impose tighter controls on armed groups have been met by violence, and it is unclear how much control the central government has over the country.

During her 1995 Washington visit, Benazir Bhutto, then prime minister of Pakistan, indicated her country's need for outside help to rein in the drug traffickers and armed sectarian groups.[54] She requested that the Clinton administration resume aid programs worth more than $600 million per annum to strengthen the government's ability to deal with these militant organizations. The Clinton administration's capacity to respond to this request, however, has been circumscribed by Pakistan's continuing efforts to develop nuclear weapons, by its support for the insurgency in Kashmir, and by the lower level of priority accorded the region after the end of the war in Afghanistan. U.S. aid to Pakistan was terminated in 1990 in compliance with the so-called Pressler amendment, which precluded U.S. foreign aid for countries actively developing nuclear weapons. Although some effort has been made to provide aircraft and equipment to Pakistan that it had long ago purchased, the issue remains bound up in nonproliferation issues.[55]

The 1990 cutoff of aid remains a source of tension with Pakistan, and is perceived by many as an indication that "the United States . . . discards allies when they no longer seem useful."[56] U.S. efforts to develop commercial relations with India have also contributed to anti-U.S. sentiment within Pakistan. India has long been Pakistan's rival in the region and has conventional forces twice the size as Pakistan's, a situation that provides impetus to Pakistan's desire to develop nuclear capability. The commercial ties are seen by many within Pakistan as proof of U.S. hostility toward the country.[57] The portrayal of the United States as anti-Islamic and pro-Indian by opposition and militant groups has further strengthened anti-U.S. sentiments. This has helped create an environment in which the more militant Islamic activists are gaining ground at the expense of traditional movements such as the Jama'at-i-Islami.

Various options have been suggested to address these issues. First, the United States could help stabilize the region by materially supporting the Pakistani government in its efforts to constrain militants and interrupt the drug trafficking that funds their operations. Second, it is suggested that U.S. policymakers should reevaluate current U.S. relations with both Pakistan and India, and should emphasize the need for evenhandedness in issues of human rights, nonproliferation, and economic and political development. While U.S. officials and many observers argue that this is currently the case, other analysts and interested parties disagree. Third, U.S. policymakers should recognize that many Pakistanis believe their country has been ill treated since the end of the Afghan war. To this end, U.S. policymakers could review the continuing relevance of the Pressler amendment, which has been argued to be counterproductive in curbing nuclear proliferation. Fourth, the development of civil society and democracy within both India and Pakistan could be supported by U.S. foreign aid expenditures. It is argued that under previous administrations, the development of independent civil institutions—particularly in Pakistan—was hindered by the fact that most U.S. aid went to the military rather than to the economy. This strengthened Pakistan's military leadership at the expense of its civilian leadership, and has had a lingering influence on the democratic development of the region. Providing economic aid—even modest amounts—might mitigate this influence. It should be noted, however, that this option remains unlikely in light of declining amounts of foreign aid allocated within the U.S. federal budget.

The situation in Afghanistan and the rise of the sectarian groups in Pakistan offers a powerful lesson about unintended consequences. The sectarian parties are, in part, a residue from the Cold War strategy of arming the *mujahidin*. The strength of these parties and the Kalashnikov culture in which they operate are both fueled by access to sophisticated weaponry left over from the war. This, in turn, is destroying the fabric of civil society in Pakistan and in other countries of the region. It is argued, then, that future policy should recognize such long-term implications and, as Paula Newberg noted, recognize that the first principle of U.S. policy should always be to "do no harm."[58]

5

TURKEY

Patricia Carley

T urkey represents an unusual case in the Islamic world, in terms both of the country's historical experience and of the ethnic origins of most of its people. Although the Turks are as resolutely Muslim as are people of Arab or Iranian descent—their Turkic Oghuz ancestors having adopted Islam as early as the seventh and eighth centuries when the Arabs invaded Central Asia—the Turks are neither Arab nor Iranian in language or ethnicity. Until the emergence of the southern republics of the former Soviet Union as independent states, Turkey was the only largely Turkic-speaking country in the world. Moreover, the Turks were never colonized, but instead established their own empire in the fifteenth century, an empire that included most of the Arab lands, among other regions. The head of that empire, the Ottoman sultan, was also the caliph—the titular head of all Muslims—and was acknowledged as such by many (though not all) of the world's Muslims even into the beginning of the twentieth century.

Perhaps the most important distinguishing feature is the legacy of Kemal Ataturk, the founder of the modern Turkish nation-state. Ataturk carved Turkey out of the ruins of the Ottoman Empire after World War I, and proceeded to establish a modern, secular state, making Turkey the first predominantly Muslim country to set up a secular political and social system. After defeating the British, French, Italian, and Greek armies occupying Anatolia, Ataturk founded the Turkish republic in 1923, and then instituted reforms designed to separate government institutions from Islamic law and clergy and to insulate the population from what he believed were some of Islam's backward influences.

Although Ataturk did not suppress Islam outright (he did not ban Islamic worship, for example), he declared that the supreme power in the new republic

79

would come from the Grand National Assembly and would not be bound by religious tenets. In 1925, *shari'a* was fully abolished and replaced by civil court, denying the clergy any influence over both criminal and private law, including marriage, divorce, and other personal matters. In 1928, Islam was stripped of its constitutional status as the official religion of the Turkish people. Also in that year, Ataturk changed the Turkish alphabet from Arabic to Latin script. Since Arabic is the language of the Qur'an, rejecting the Arabic script served to further distance the Turkish people from their Islamic heritage.

One of the aims of Ataturk's reforms was to give the new country a Western orientation. Although it was not until after World War II that Turkey officially joined the Western bloc, Ataturk was determined that his new Turkish nation would be a European state. He was wholly uninterested in ideologies such as pan-Turkism or pan-Islamism, which he believed would, among other things, draw Turkey toward the Islamic East and away from the modern world of nation-states. Given his determination to secularize Turkey, he had little interest in preserving ties with other Islamic peoples, or, for that matter, in pursuing new ties with the rest of the world's Turkic peoples (most of whom were then in the Soviet Union). In the aftermath of World War II, when Stalin made bellicose demands on the Bosphorus Straits and on Turkey's eastern territory, the Turks became more solidly pro-Western by joining the newly formed NATO security alliance. Since then, Turkey has been a steadfast and important ally of the West, particularly the United States, and one of the largest recipients of American foreign aid.

These two principles, secularism and Western orientation, have remained as foundations of the Turkish republic since Ataturk's death in 1938, and they have done much to shape public and especially official attitudes in Turkey toward the role of religion in politics. However, attitudes toward Islam and secularism in Turkey have not remained static, nor are they the same throughout the country. While it was fashionable, until very recently, for Westernized Turks devoted to Ataturk and his principles to eschew all religious influence in public life, many other Turks, especially among the rural population, retained their traditional attachment to Islam. Thus, something of a dichotomy developed within Turkish society between largely secularized urban elites and more traditionally minded people in the countryside.

Secularism was doubtlessly controversial among much of the population in Ataturk's time, and remains so with some segments today. Not long after Ataturk's death, those persons particularly unhappy with the radical changes implemented by Ataturk rallied around the Democrat Party led by Adnan Menderes, who pledged to loosen the restraints on Islamic practice and influence in society. Capitalizing also on general economic distress, Menderes became prime minister in 1950, and proceeded to roll back some of Ataturk's reforms. He allowed the call to prayer in Arabic (Ataturk had declared that all prayers must be in Turkish), Qur'anic recitations on state radio, the use of state funds to build thousands of new mosques, and the reopening of a number of religious schools.

The republican establishment—particularly the military and the foreign ministry—were alarmed by Menderes's actions and, in 1960, the military, proclaiming the need to defend Ataturkism, staged the first of its coups against civilian leaders. Menderes and two other leaders of the Democrat Party were hanged for treason, a charge based primarily on the party's rollback of Ataturk's secularist policies. This period revealed the divisions within Turkish society: Menderes was supported largely by those least affected by the changes in Turkish society—the peasants—and was strongly opposed and eventually deposed by the institutions most committed to preserving Ataturkist principles, primarily secularism. This urban-rural and elite-peasant split is no longer as clear-cut as was the case earlier, however, as millions of Turkish peasants have moved to the cities in recent decades, and increasing numbers of government bureaucrats have become ambivalent about the principle of secularism.

European attitudes toward the Turks may have fueled the desire of many Turks to reconnect with their Islamic past. Turkey has sought for decades to become more officially integrated into Western Europe, and first applied to join the (then) European Economic Community more than thirty years ago. However, its applications have been consistently rejected, and not always for principled reasons. Officially, the justifications have included European concerns over Turkey's continued human rights problems in dealing with its large Kurdish minority. Unofficially, however, Turks have been made to feel that, as Muslims, they simply can never expect to be accepted as Europeans, a situation that clearly stirs Turkish resentment and is exacerbated by the ill-treatment of Turkish migrant workers in several Western European countries. The Turks, who consider themselves to be the successors of a great Islamic empire, have reacted with increasing anger, causing some openly to question the wisdom of Turkey's Western orientation. Consequently, in the debate in the European Parliament over Turkey's application for membership in the European Customs Union, arguments were frequently made that a rejection would be sure to fan

Islamist forces in Turkey. Turkey's application for membership was approved on December 12, 1995.

It is against this background that the role of Islam in contemporary Turkish society and politics must be understood. Not long after the Institute's meeting on Turkey, parliamentary elections were held in that country. In these elections, held in December 1995, the Islam-based Refah (Welfare) party received the most votes (though just barely), 21.4 percent. The two center-right parties, the True Path Party (DYP) and the Motherland Party (ANAP), received slightly smaller percentages, 19.2 percent and 19.6 percent, respectively. Two center-left parties also received significant percentages: the Democratic Left Party (DSP), 14.6 percent, and the Republican People's Party (CHP), 10.7 percent. Refah's win, however close, was an extremely notable development, because it was the first time in Turkish history that a party expressly opposed to secularism gained the largest number of votes. In addition to its hostility to secularism, the Refah party, led by Necmettin Erbakan, had pledged to reexamine Turkey's relationship with the West, including its membership in NATO.

It should be pointed out that neither Erbakan nor an Islam-based party is new to Turkey's political scene. To the contrary, Erbakan has been a fixture in Turkish politics at least since 1972, when he founded the National Salvation Party (NSP), essentially the precursor to the Refah party, which routinely gained anywhere from 5 percent to 12 percent of the vote in the 1970s. After a military coup in 1980, Erbakan was banned from politics, along with numerous other familiar political leaders (including the current president, Suleyman Demirel), until the ban was lifted in 1987. Thus, unlike many other Muslim countries, Turkey has allowed participation of the Islamic-oriented parties in politics or, at the very least, such parties have not been singled out exclusively for harassment.

It is of course not yet clear what the surge in the popularity of the Refah party will mean in Turkey's political future and its relations with the West. Even before the election, Refah leader Erbakan had relaxed his stance against the West, and stated that no radical changes would be implemented quickly. In addition, many observers—and even Refah leaders—acknowledged that a vote for Refah was as much a protest vote against both the DYP and the ANAP, which have alternately controlled the government for the past decade, as a vote in favor of any major changes in the policy of secularism. It may also be the case that whatever enthusiasm for Islamic activism may have existed in Turkey has since waned in the aftermath of the Iranian revolution. Nonetheless, it is increasingly apparent that the dichotomy in Turkish society between government elites and the less modernized, more traditional parts of society can no longer be ignored.

After the December 1995 elections, Turkey experienced considerable difficulty in establishing a stable ruling coalition. Initially, despite its having received the largest number of votes, Refah was unable to convince either of the other major parties to join in forming a government. Bitter rivalries prevented the two center-right parties, the DYP and the ANAP, from forming a minority government for several months, until a shaky compromise arrangement was agreed to in March 1996. That coalition collapsed after only three months, however, and the reins were handed back to Erbakan to try again. DYP leader Tansu Ciller, in a somewhat surprising reversal, agreed to accept a coalition with Refah and, in July 1996, the two parties established Turkey's first-ever Islamist-led government.

Significantly, after being named prime minister, Erbakan softened his anti-Western positions even more and reaffirmed Turkey's status as a secular and democratic state. Perhaps most notably, Erbakan, who had been hostile to Ataturkism for much of his political life, paid homage to the country's founder by visiting his tomb in the manner customary for all new prime ministers. However, there remains uncertainty among many in and outside Turkey about his true goals for the country, something that became more apparent after two major foreign visits he took as prime minister. In August 1996, Erbakan visited Iran, where he signed a $20 billion natural gas deal with the Iranian government. In the wake of considerable American alarm at the trip as well as concern inside Turkey, Erbakan claimed that his visit was taken not for ideological reasons but to augment Turkey's natural gas supply.

The following October, with the aim of strengthening ties to other Islamic countries, the Turkish prime minister visited Egypt, Libya, and Nigeria, in spite of the latter two countries' status in Western eyes as rogue states. The stop in Libya proved most controversial for Erbakan, as Libyan leader Muammar Qaddhafi reproached his Turkish visitors for their repression of the Kurds. The Turkish public was outraged, and the incident prompted a confidence vote in the Turkish parliament (which Erbakan survived). It is not clear whether Erbakan was sufficiently chastened by the Libya visit to cool his pursuit of relations with the Islamic world, or at least its outlaw members. He himself remained unrepentant about his trip, though was likely mindful of the anger it generated among the Turkish population.

Since then, many in Turkey have become concerned to the point of alarm at the increasing number of Islamic activist actions (the strengthening of Islamic schools, the wearing of Islamic dress, and the growth of Islam-oriented television stations, for example) that directly challenge the policy of secularism and, in some cases, the country's secularist laws. In February 1997, the National Security Council issued a call for Islam to be kept out of public life, and made clear that the government must work harder to contain such activities and to prosecute those who violate laws protecting secularism. Erbakan reluctantly agreed to the National Security Council's demands, though it remains to be seen what kind of effort will be made to implement them.

TURKEY IS DIFFERENT

Even in view of the recent success of the Refah party, the question still remains: Why has Islamic activism not been as strong and violent a force in Turkey as in some other Islamic countries? Serif Mardin of American University stated simply that Turkey is different. As a result of the secular system created by Ataturk (which survived after his death) and the role of the bureaucracy in the Ottoman Empire and in modern Turkey, religion and political power have always been in an "unequal equilibrium." The state structure and bureaucracy have always had more political power than the religious institutions. This situation is in contrast to other Muslim societies, in both the past and the present, where the clergy, as the interpreters of the *shari'a*, were not as subservient to the state and its establishments as they were in the Ottoman Empire.

Mardin also noted the importance of personal identity in Turkey, of the "construction of the self," as uniquely shading the way Turks see themselves and their world. This identity construction, which is now a greater problem than it was before modernization, has different dimensions in the Turkish and Arab worlds. For example, a "layering" exists in the minds of Turks: They are proud of their Islamic tradition and of their association with the conquering Ottoman Empire, but at the same time they desire to be part of Western, modernized Europe. These feelings exist together and, to a Turk, they represent no contradiction at all. Nor do Turks see why their former Islamic and Ottoman traditions should disqualify them from becoming full members of Europe.

Graham Fuller of the RAND Corporation suggested that perhaps Islam in Turkey is different from Islam in other countries because of Turkey's greater political development over the past decades, particularly its adoption of

Western political institutions. If it is true that Turkey, with all its difficulties, does have legitimate and functioning democratic institutions, then it is not surprising that the kind of Islam that exists there reflects this. Islam in Turkey may simply be more democratic. Furthermore, Islamic movements in Turkey do not have to contend with the resentments over Western imperialism, which are a significant source of support for Islamic movements elsewhere. Therefore, even if an Islamic party were to come to power in Turkey, it might be more likely to emphasize moderate cultural and societal reform than the strict revolutionary application of *shari'a* linked with hostility toward the West.

THE REFAH PARTY IN TURKISH POLITICS

The Refah party was formed in the latter part of the 1980s by Erbakan after the ban was lifted on his participation in politics. For a time, the Islam-oriented political party was allied with the conservative Nationalist Work Party led by Alparslan Turkes, an alliance that enabled Turkes's party to get nineteen representatives voted into parliament in the 1991 elections. After those elections, Turkes slowly disengaged from the alliance (Turkes has since died) and Refah became stronger in its own right. Refah's platform, among other things, has questioned Turkey's Western orientation, its determination to gain membership in the European Union, and its adoption of Western banking practices. However, many of the party's stances have been modified at various times, not the least just before and immediately after the December 1995 elections.

Although too much is often made of Refah in the West, Morton Abramowitz of the Carnegie Endowment maintained that it has many strengths the other political parties lack. "Refah has money, purpose, an alternate vision for Turks which has not yet been tested, and more than thirty years of electoral experience in various incarnations." Refah also has a "nationalist ethos" that includes anti-Westernism and a modern-oriented membership of people with considerable government experience. But perhaps Refah's strongest advantage is the increasing ineffectiveness of Turkey's other political parties, a process of deterioration that began in 1989, when President Turgut Ozal put Yildirim Akbulut in power as prime minister. Despite having Akbulut as prime minister, Ozal himself retained real state power, thereby blurring constitutional distinctions that relegate the president to a more ceremonial role, and undermining political parties. Abramowitz claimed that since that time, there have been no significant achievements by any of Turkey's succeeding governments, except perhaps some successes in foreign affairs. It is the inability of the Turkish political system to produce effective governments that will probably be the main factor that determines Refah's continued success.

The Refah party does, however, have its weaknesses. Abramowitz quoted a conversation with President Ozal that took place not long before the former president died in April 1993. Ozal conceded that Refah might survive as part of a coalition government. But if it were to come to power outright, it would, first and foremost, have to diminish the hostility of the Turkish military. Beyond that, it would need to get rid of Erbakan, as he is simply out of step with the times and too much of a liability in Turkish politics. Refah would also need to develop a coherent economic program, control the factionalism in the party and the wide differences in ideology, and restrain certain anti-Semitic tendencies. The Refah party would need to do more than merely depend on the failure of the current political parties to ensure its future success.

It is generally accepted by most experts on Turkey that, although there are Islamic activists and sympathizers in Turkey, many, if not most, of the people who currently support Refah do so for economic rather than ideological reasons. People simply want economic change, and there is a definite lack of confidence in the ruling parties' ability—or willingness—to bring that about. According to Heath Lowry of Princeton University, economic conditions for many in Turkey have become extremely bad, and the secular parties, especially those on the center-right that have held power for the last decade, have not addressed the problem. After all, "refah" in Turkish can be translated not only as "welfare," but also as "prosperity," which Refah promises to bring to the poorer segments of Turkish society. This is not merely political rhetoric, Lowry suggested. The Refah party has set up an infrastructure throughout the country through which it provides for the needs of some of Turkey's poorest people, especially peasants from Anatolia who are new arrivals to the cities. No other political party has made any attempt to help this segment of the population.

In addition, Lowry continued, many who support the party do so because it has not been tried—until recently, Refah had not been part of the government for almost twenty years. Few voters remember the last time Erbakan's party (then called the National Salvation Party) played a political role. In addition, as Sabri Sayari of the Institute for Turkish Studies pointed out, Refah has an increasingly large presence in Turkey's media, especially television. By the start of 1996, Refah owned three major national television stations and many more local stations throughout the country. In some towns, the Refah-owned channel is the only local one.

ISLAMIC LIFE OUTSIDE REFAH

Sufi Brotherhoods

It is important to remember that Islam in Turkey is not monolithic—it is more than just the Refah party. Islam in Turkish society is also distinguished by the existence of intermediary organizations of a special religious type. To understand Islamic politics in Turkey it is necessary to see what goes on at the community level (or *cemaat*, in Turkish). In the United States, the Refah party is often seen as the political carrier of Islamic activism, and it certainly gets the most attention. Yet, according to Serif Mardin, Islamic life in Turkey is made up of many small subgroups, some, but not all, of which maintain allegiance to Refah.

Sufi orders are one example of such intermediary organizations, and Islam's role in Turkish politics cannot be understood without taking these groups into account. One of the most important of these communities is the Nakshibandi Sufi order, which, since the eighteenth century, has become an organization for mobilizing Muslims in Turkey and throughout the Muslim world. The Nakshibandi order has traditionally activated believers in a spiritual sense by bringing them back to their true religion, and in a political sense by leading the fight against colonialism and other foreign influences. They order has continued to play this role in Turkey, by training and educating Muslims, particularly in the eastern regions of the country. Although not necessarily Kurdish themselves, the Nakshibandis became teachers in the Kurdish regions of the Ottoman Empire during the nineteenth century and, since that time, they have had a significant influence in those regions as community leaders and organizers. The situation is even more complicated by the fact that Nakshibandis themselves are not unified. There are six or seven subgroups, some of which support Refah and others of which support the DYP, or even the conservative Great Unity Party. Some of these smaller Nakshibandi groups own hospitals, media organs, or other active investments in the community.

Religious Schools

In recent years, there has been a large jump in enrollment in Islamic schools in Turkey, although it is not clear whether there is any direct connection between this development and growing support for the Refah party. According to Mardin, there are currently 448 religious schools in Turkey (which have been allowed to exist only since 1951). Of those schools, approximately half have been registered only since 1990; 38 schools have been built by the state, 77 by the state and private citizens together, and fully 258 by private citizens alone. Turks are, apparently, increasingly willing to pay for such schooling for their children.

However, it is not clear that the graduates of these Islamic schools are producing Refah adherents. Mardin noted that there has been an increasing number of complaints from former students in these schools about the burden of studying both religious and secular subjects. Since the schools are not sufficiently focused, the complaints go, even with diplomas, their schooling has not made the students eligible to become religious teachers, or imams, nor do they have enough qualifications to enter university. Thus, although some point to the increasing number of Islamic schools in Turkey as a source of the growing popularity of Refah, these schools are not as popular as many believe. They may, in fact, not be the Refah recruiting grounds that some consider them to be.

Refah and the Policy of Secularism

Abramowitz contended that Ataturkism is in retreat in Turkey. As a matter of fact, it never had a great deal of effect on the rural people, whether in the countryside or increasingly in the cities, where vast numbers have migrated and which have generally been the base of Islam-oriented parties. "Certainly Islam is a major aspect of Turkish life, and it is hard to envision a democratic Turkey without religious parties," Abramowitz said. At the same time, religion is one of the most exploited issues in Turkey, and all political parties have used it, at one time or another, to further their own domestic political aims.

According to Lowry, most Turks believe that many, if not all, of the foundations of the modern Turkish republic are associated with secularism, particularly modernization and Westernization. Rejection of secularism is essentially a rejection of these two tenets, and, more practically, of membership in NATO. Abrogating it would entail a significant change in Turkey's fifty-year relationship with the West, particularly the United States. To most observers of Turkey, the commitment to secularism is so fundamental to Turkish life that any attempt to deny it (or, for that matter, to pull Turkey out of NATO) would cause the Turkish military to reassert itself politically, a move that would "set Turkey back fifty years" in economic and political terms.

Regardless of whether secularism is on the wane in Turkey, the strict implementation of that policy throughout this century, according to Lowry, has resulted in the crippling of "high" or formal Islam in Turkey. Furthermore, although Islam was in no way destroyed at the "folk" level, it was certainly repressed to a great extent. No other Islamic country was affected in this way. Today, a strange "hybrid" is now "coming out of the ground" at both the folk and formal levels, a development that may account for the distinctive quality of the Islamic movement in Turkey.

It must be admitted that there has recently been Islamic-based violence in Turkey, Sayari noted. Several intellectuals known especially for their strong advocacy of secularism have been assassinated in recent years. However, the violence has thus far not been linked to Refah, which condemns the killings. It is also clandestine, and rarely do the perpetrators make themselves known or ever get caught. Rumors abound about the underground Islamic groups' ties to Iran, but this association has never been proven.

The Alevi Community

One special aspect of Islam in Turkey is the large Alevi minority that resides mainly in central Anatolia. Although Turkey is often described as a Sunni Muslim country, the Alevi community is Shi'ite and it makes up over 20 percent of the population. According to Henri Barkey of Lehigh University, the Alevis have traditionally been some of the strongest supporters of secularism in Turkey, primarily because, as Shi'ites, they fear what might happen under an assertive Sunni government. Partly because of this fear, the Alevis are highly politicized and well organized. A Refah government that attempted to roll back secularism would provoke a strong reaction from the sizable Alevi community.

A REFAH GOVERNMENT: WHAT WOULD CHANGE?

While a Refah government would be unlikely to directly attack the major foundations of Turkish political life, including secularism, it could be expected, according to Alan Makovsky of the Washington Institute for Near East Policy, to take smaller steps in that direction. In 1995, for example, Refah announced that it would seek a change in Article 24 of the Constitution, which enshrines secularism in the country. This move apparently found much resonance among Muslims in other parties. Ironically, "church" and state are not exactly separate in Turkey—the state controls religion through the Religious Affairs Directorate (the Diyanet)—and there are numerous Refah supporters in the directorate already. This institution, although relatively small, could do much to chip away at Turkey's secularist foundations, even if its Refah members never get as far as to establish *shariʿa*.

In any case, while some observers do not find cause for alarm if Refah should attain full power in Turkey (as opposed to becoming part of a coalition), others worry that such a development could spell disaster for that country, at least in the short term. A Refah government, Abramowitz contended, would change the way Europeans view Turkey, particularly in political and economic terms. Decisions about foreign investment would be radically affected, and there would be concern that Refah's revolutionary instincts would lead it to overturn the way Turkey is governed, including its Western orientation. With Refah in full control, Turkey's application for membership in the European Union would undoubtedly be set back several decades.

Lowry pointed out that Refah has successfully permeated key parts of the Turkish bureaucracy. The Ministry of the Interior, for example, is now said to be heavily staffed with people of religious orientation, as is the Ministry of Education. In fact, if Refah has done so well when it has not been part of the system, how much more could it accomplish if it were to become a dominant player, with the ability to control the machinery of government?

However, it is probable that the Turkish Islamic activists' involvement in politics and government has produced some moderation and possibly a more pragmatic approach to governing than might be found among Muslim parties in other countries. As Barkey pointed out, only a few weeks before the December 24, 1995, election, Refah suddenly changed its position on Turkey's membership in the European Customs Union. Previously, the party had been categorically opposed; however, in the weeks of furious campaigning prior to the election, Refah announced that it would support Turkey's membership in the customs union, though with modifications. Similarly, Sayari pointed out that after three decades of condemning usury (*ṛais*), Refah announced that it would accept the terms of the existing system in Turkey. Of greatest interest to U.S. policymakers is the fact, generally agreed on by most observers in and outside Turkey, that whatever the rhetoric, Refah would probably be incapable of altering Turkey's membership in NATO.

Changes would, however, in all likelihood occur in Turkey's foreign policy, especially in regard to the Middle East. Alan Makovsky suggested that Refah would probably attempt to take a decidedly less friendly position toward Israel, and accentuate the Islamic component (as opposed to ethnic identity or language) in its relations with the Central Asian countries. He also maintained that such moves would make it more difficult for Turkey's supporters to champion it as a democratic, pro-Western, and secular country, an occurrence that would have a significant effect on Turkey's overall foreign relations. One point is absolutely clear, according to Lowry: If any attempt were made to thwart the Refah party's election victory by preventing it from assuming the power it gained democratically, then there would be bloodshed in Turkey.

U.S. POLICY

Western knowledge about Islam in Turkey has tended to be superficial. Despite the commitment to secularism, mixing religion and politics is not a new phenomenon in Turkey. It has been around at least since 1950 with the advent of the Democrat Party under Adnan Menderes. The United States should therefore be more accustomed to seeing this mixture as a normal element of Turkish political life.

Throughout the late 1980s, the United States did not do enough to understand religion in Turkey or the role of the Refah party. In fact, according to Abramowitz, the U.S. embassy in Turkey did not stay in contact with Refah for fear of sending the wrong signal to the Turks. Consequently, the United States does not know much about Refah, a problem that has grown worse as the party has become more powerful. The U.S. embassy could correct this deficiency by making itself available to senior Refah leaders on a cordial and businesslike basis, but without giving the impression that it favors Refah. Granted, this will be a delicate task, as it risks alienating some other Turkish groups, but not much is gained by avoiding Refah. In any case, the greatest concern should be finding ways to halt the general decline of Turkey's political system.

According to Sayari, there are some curious contradictions in Turkish attitudes toward the United States that affect what the United States can do. As outrageous as it may seem, some in the Turkish secular press believe that the United States is directly responsible for the rise of Islam in Turkey—that rise being an outgrowth of U.S. support for Islamic forces throughout the world in the fight against communism (as in Afghanistan, for example). Conversely, Islamic activists see the United States as a major obstacle to the changes they would like to see happen.

Samuel Lewis pointed out two possible scenarios that would leave the United States with a particularly unwelcome policy dilemma. One has Refah coming to power outright and democratically changing Turkey's foreign policy orientation. The other envisions a military intervention to prevent the Refah party from forming a government. Neither of these alternatives is seen to be in the best interests of either the United States or Turkey. The second scenario may protect U.S. interests in the short term—Turkey's membership in NATO, for example—but it would also go against many American principles and be disastrous for Turkey's relations with Western Europe. The real difficulty is that a policy of passivity, which may have worked in Algeria, would be unimaginable toward an ally as important as Turkey.

Whether the West likes it or not, the Refah party is a reality in Turkey; it cannot be wished away. Its strength is clearly growing and, so far, this process has taken place through democratic means. According to Fuller, the United States will have to live with the party and its aspirations. Turkish politics must be allowed to take its course, and Refah given the chance to succeed or fail. Otherwise, Refah will continue to be seen as the only alternative—and a "pure," uncorrupted one at that. Any American effort to inhibit Refah's prospects would be very ill advised.

CONCLUSION

"Turkey is not the Refah party," Mardin concluded. Turkey is a democracy and it functions as the sum of many forces, including government, the judiciary, free press, public opinion, the military, universities, and so on. If Refah ever does come to full power in Turkey, like other parties it will have to take all of these forces into consideration. That is an important difference between Turkey and Algeria, because Algeria has always lacked these other forces, except for the military.

The conflict between the Refah party and those groups it opposes is not so much political or even ideological. It is a class conflict, or at least a class conflict in the limited sense of urban-rural differences, although these differences are increasingly less marked because of the rural migration to the cities. Nonetheless, members of the Refah party continue to see themselves as a repressed group, discriminated against on the basis of their Muslim identity, and to see others as their oppressors. This is a recipe for growing tension, and leaves open the possibility of great social strife.

The threat to the West from Refah may, in the final analysis, be overblown. According to Mardin, nothing, not even a Refah government, is going to change the fact that 60 percent of Turkey's trade is with Western Europe. Given this reality, Turkish politics, including the political role of Islam and attitudes of Islamic activists toward the West, will have only a limited impact on Turkey's future and its place in the international community. Moreover, Turkey's democratic institutions have proven to be highly resilient, even in the face of direct threats to the system. Islam in Turkey is not necessarily about Islamic fundamentalism in some general sense, but about the specific history of Islam in Turkey and how it shapes—and is shaped by—the Turkish people and their distinct history and traditions.

INDONESIA

I ndonesia is the world's largest Islamic country, with close to 90 percent of its 193 million people officially registered as Muslim.[1] The country has not, however, been plagued in recent years with the kind of religious extremism, violence, and intolerance that are present in other areas examined by this study. On the contrary, Suharto's New Order regime, which has ruled Indonesia since the 1960s, has based its tenure on the twin pillars of national unity and religious pluralism, even if it has relied upon repression and military rule to enforce these policies. Consequently, when the Institute working group members[2] were asked whether or not Indonesia is in danger of "turning fundamentalist" or is under threat from a militant Islamic insurgency, the answer was a uniform "no."

Although there does not appear to be a significant "threat" of Islamic extremism in the conventional sense, the centrality of Islam in Indonesian politics has been increasing over the last decade. This is the result of, first, a distinctly stronger sense of Islamic identity among Indonesians, and, second, the Suharto regime's increasing use of Islam as a means of supporting its rule. While the overall trend is clear, the implications remained less so. Many Indonesians (and Western analysts) are concerned that this "greening" of Indonesian politics may fuel intercommunal tensions and threaten the country's tradition of religious tolerance.

HISTORY

Islam in Indonesia has traditionally been characterized by a tolerance of diversity and of religious minorities. In some respects, it had to be; though predominantly Muslim, Indonesia's large population represents a diversity drawn from three hundred different cultures in the archipelago of sixteen thousand islands. Islam originally came to Indonesia in the fifteenth century as a result not of armed invasion, but of contact with South Asian traders. The new religion merged with the local cultures and older (Hindu) belief systems to create a syncretic and adaptable version of Islam. Strong Sufi influence—particularly the tolerance for local customs—facilitated the spread of Islam. A more orthodox interpretation of Islam became better known and more influential in Indonesia by the eighteenth century, reflecting a shift in the dominant "external influences on Indonesian Islam . . . from its former center on the Indian subcontinent to the Middle East."[3] These two trends continue to coexist today. Adherents to the syncretic form of Islam are known as abangan or "nominal" Muslims, while members of the other group are known as santri or "orthodox" Muslims.

The Dutch colonial presence in the then–East Indies formally began in 1799, though it was not until 1910 that the military conquest of the archipelago was completed.[4] The European rulers established an economic and legal infrastructure that provided differing rights and duties based on a "form of racial classification."[5] Christians, both European and those of Chinese descent, benefited disproportionately from the situation. For example, the Chinese, though precluded from owning property, came to dominate small- and medium-scale commerce, to the detriment of native Indonesians. "The Catholics and Protestants were the favored children of the colonial rulers."[6]

As in other colonized states, the early twentieth century saw the rise of various nationalist movements. Sarekat Islam, an Islamic group established in 1912, was one of the first mass nationalist organizations, and was particularly influential through the early 1920s. "Given the great ethnic and linguistic diversity across the archipelago, Islam provided the one common thread for the vast majority of the population. It differentiated the Indonesians from their Christian masters and gave them a sense of identity with a universal cause."[7] The Islamic movement, however, divided over religious differences, giving rise to the traditionalist Nahdatul Ulama (established in 1926) and, after the demise of the Sarekat Islam, to a more influential Muhammadiyah, a modernist social and educational organization that had coexisted with Sarekat Islam since 1912. It was, however, the secular nationalists who ultimately emerged as the dominant opposition to colonial rule, though the weak position of their movements kept them from achieving much. It was only with the Japanese occupation during World War II that Dutch control was removed.

In the aftermath of the Japanese surrender to the Allied forces in 1945, Indonesia declared independence. After four years of fighting and negotiation, the Dutch bowed to international—and particularly U.S.—pressure and formally transferred sovereignty to the Indonesian nationalists in 1949.

Debate over the role of Islam in the new state was an early source of tension. An agreement among the various nationalist factions to incorporate the *shari'a* and other Islamic elements into a constitution was abrogated in favor of a more pluralist and secularist approach to religion in the new state. The subsequent provisional constitutions adopted in 1949 and 1950 did not change this, despite pressure from some Islamic activists who wanted to create an Islamic state.

The secularist interpretation was advocated by abangan Muslims and non-Muslims who—out of concern for national unity—opposed defining national identity in religious terms. Instead, the constitution offered an alternative: a secular state (that is, no established religion) based on the five principles known as *Pancasila:* belief in God, national unity, consensus through deliberation, humanitarianism, and social justice.

It is argued that the politics of this early period reflected the traditional abangan-santri split, and would significantly influence the early policies of the New Order regime. First, the independence movement against Dutch colonial rule prior to World War II, though fragmented along religious and ethnic lines, was dominated by secular nationalists, composed largely of abangans and non-Muslims. The military from the colonial period on had been similarly dominated by abangan Muslims and non-Muslims, and were opposed to Indonesia's becoming an Islamic state. Finally, it is argued that by the 1950s "anti-Islamic attitudes [had] crystallized in large portions of the political elite, including the military."[8] Islam had come to be perceived as "parochial and backward, a part of Indonesia's past rather than its future."[9]

INDEPENDENCE, THE NEW ORDER, AND ISLAM

The period from 1950 to 1957 was one of weak parliamentary democracy, characterized by shifting coalitions, partisan discord, and an inability of the country to deal with the problems left over from the colonial era. Free elections held in 1955 saw the electorate mobilized along ethnic and religious lines, with no single group able to attain a significant majority. The country faced a number of regional rebellions in the mid-1950s, including a militant insurgency by radical Muslims who opposed the secular polices of the central government and who wished to establish an Islamic state. Martial law was established in 1957 by President Sukarno, though fighting would continue until 1959. The left-leaning Sukarno continued to rule Indonesia until 1966.

A failed coup attempt by a group of junior military officers in 1965—allegedly with the knowledge of both the Indonesian Communist Party (PKI) and President Sukarno—set in motion a series of events that culminated in the downfall of Sukarno. Army Strategic Forces Commander Major General Suharto succeeded Sukarno as the president of Indonesia and established the "New Order" with the support of the armed services and a broad coalition of Muslim and other organizations. The Muslim groups had vehemently opposed the communist influence under Sukarno, not least because of the PKI's hostility to Islam, but also in part because of the participation of large landowning families in Islamic groups. At first there were hopes of a real power-sharing arrangement under this new situation, but "by the end of the decade . . . it had become clear that the New Order was an authoritarian military regime"[10] and had no desire to share power with anyone.

The treatment of Islamic political activists under the New Order has fluctuated significantly. Although initially allied with various Muslim groups, Suharto carried out a harsh policy of repression against religiously based political activism. Muslim activists, perceived as supporters of the regional rebellions of the 1950s, were viewed with suspicion by the military government. Though the regime's real animus was directed toward the communist party, Islamic political activists were considered "public enemy number two." They were labeled extremists and "discriminated against, persecuted, arrested on seemingly flimsy charges, and sometimes given lengthy jail sentences."[11] Suspected Islamic activists were barred from holding government positions, and their interests were not represented in the parliament.

The four Islamic parties that had participated in the 1955 elections were eventually forced to form one political party, the Development Unity Party (PPP). The PPP was later forced to drop Islamic references from its name, change its ballot symbol—formerly the Ka'bah shrine in Mecca—and, in the early 1980s, along with all other social organizations, adopt *Pancasila* as its sole ideological basis.

At the same time, however, Suharto sought to use religion as a means of strengthening his rule. Although political expression of religion remained tightly curtailed, the New Order encouraged personal piety and religious practice in an effort to oppose communism. Atheism, which was closely associated with the communist party, was outlawed on the grounds that it was inconsistent with *Pancasila*. Furthermore, "students in all schools, public and private, and at all levels were required to take instruction in the religion of their parents' choice."[12]

This compulsory religious education had a profound impact on the Islamization of Indonesian society. Along with the mandatory religious education came significant financial resources that rapidly expanded the state school system. Coupled with the successful economic development that has marked Indonesia in recent times, the result has been "a more uniformly Islamic population and a growing Islamic middle class." It is within this context that the Association of Islamic Intellectuals (ICMI) was established by the Suharto regime in the early 1990s as a tool to facilitate his next election.

INSTITUTE MEETING

In his opening remarks at the Institute meeting, William Liddle of Ohio State University set out to clarify what he termed "the political map of Indonesian Islam." He called attention to the divisions of Indonesian Muslims into the santri and the abangan,[13] and further subdivided the santri into modernists and traditionalists. Modernists tend to be urban traders, and typically non-Javanese, while most traditionalists are from rural areas and more influenced by Javanese culture.

While the validity today of these analytical divisions remains a source of debate, Liddle argued that the conceptual framework remains important in understanding Islamic politics in Indonesia. Conceding that the divisions are in fact breaking down, these different groups have formed, and continue to serve loosely as, the basis of the major political and social organizations within Indonesia.[14] In the immediate postwar years, the modernists found political expression through the Masjumi political party (dominated by the Muhammadiyah),[15] and the traditionalists were represented by Nahdatul Ulama (NU). The abangan Muslims dominated the nationalist parties and the Communist Party. Government restrictions on political activities, including outright bans on certain groups, limited the effectiveness of those groups representing the santri Muslims, as well as the communists.

The military, Suharto's base of support, has traditionally been dominated by abangan Muslims and non-Muslims.[16] It has been a staunch supporter of the secular basis of Indonesian government, and has had an extensive role within both government administration and electoral politics. The state political party, Golkar (literally, "functional groups"), has been tied closely to the military as well as to the state bureaucracy. The party has dominated electoral politics since its inception in 1969, and has served as a vehicle for Suharto's massive electoral victories in a series of less-than-fair elections since 1971. Golkar is, basically, "the partisan face of [Suharto's] armed forces/civilian bureaucracy power base."[17]

The creation of ICMI, however, represents an apparent shift in government policy toward these different groups. First, in light of the regime's past policies toward Muslim activists, the creation of ICMI marks a significant change in government policy away from repression and toward a policy of active co-optation.[18] Modernist intellectuals, Islamic activists, and others have coalesced around ICMI, seeing it as a vehicle for legitimate political participation. Second, Suharto has promoted generals of santri background into leadership positions within the armed services, apparently in an effort to isolate one of his main rivals, General Murdani (a Roman Catholic), and those who support Murdani. Finally, it is argued that ICMI is being used by Suharto to strengthen the regime's standing among more devout Muslims in anticipation of elections scheduled for 1997 and 1998. The appointment of key Golkar figures to head ICMI would seem to reinforce this point.

While the rise of ICMI reflects "the new centrality of Islam in Indonesian public life,"[19] the extent of any real change in attitude of the Suharto regime toward Islam is qualified by three factors: (1) the Suharto regime's control and financing of ICMI, (2) the organization's membership, and (3) its message.

On the first factor, ICMI remains under the control of state officials beholden to Suharto, and led by Suharto's minister of research and technology, B. J. Habibie. As regards the second factor, of the two most influential groups within the organization—namely, the technocratic elite and the social activists—it is the former that is said to dominate. This group, which is arguably the inheritor of the modernist tradition, includes high-skilled professionals and government bureaucrats affiliated with the state-run heavy industries, and seeks to link its Islamic religious beliefs with participation in the modern world. Members of this group are devout Muslims whose interpretation of Islam has little to do with politics or foreign policy.

As for the third factor, although ICMI is an explicitly Islamic organization, its dominant theme is human resource development, not Islamic theology. This approach appears to target two significant constituencies. The organization's

Islamic identity has a broad appeal among the majority of Indonesians, while the substantive emphasis on human resource development resonates most strongly with those in government and industry. "Organizational themes like developmentalism, professionalism, and Islam serve a number of purposes. For insiders, they are a kind of normative or ideological glue, providing a larger sense of purpose than mere aggrandizement of bureaucratic power would do. Toward outsiders, they are employed to attract support or to neutralize potential opposition."[20]

The question remains, however, who is co-opting whom? If the government's goal is to strengthen its Islamic credentials through ICMI, the activists—the second largest group in ICMI—seek to use the organization to influence government policy on social and economic issues.[21] Previously excluded from New Order politics, these activists have been successful in forcing changes in long-standing government policies. Such changes include the establishment of an Islamic bank, the elimination of a ban on women wearing Islamic head-covering (hijab) in state schools, the codification of Islamic family law, new restrictions on interfaith marriage, and the elimination of a national sports lottery.

Is this trend disturbing? Possibly not. It is unlikely that the government will suddenly turn hostile to the West. On the contrary, most of the Institute participants agreed that there is little inconsistency between Indonesia's policies and U.S. interests in the region. However, there remains legitimate concern among minority groups and others about the danger of increased religious and ethnic tensions resulting from ICMI actions.

Indonesians of Chinese descent, who are predominantly Christian, fear the development of intercommunal tensions. Although the ethnic Chinese make up only about 5 percent of the population, they control a significant share of Indonesia's business life. Consequently, there is real concern that tensions based on wide disparities in income and social position may manifest themselves in Christian-Muslim terms. There are already young "would-be activists" who recognize the effectiveness of using Islamic symbols to mobilize the poor for political ends. The ICMI-supported newspaper, Republika, has run articles that criticize "capitalist exploitation of the urban and rural poor" and display "religious and racial undertones."[22]

Sidney Jones of Human Rights Watch/Asia affirmed the validity of these concerns. In her recent trips to the country, she witnessed increased interfaith tension, or, as she phrased it, an assertive "nationalist Muslim sentiment." This tension is due in no small part to the climate created by ICMI. Pointing to

several specific examples, Jones indicated how local conflicts, although not necessarily about religious matters, were redefined at the national level in terms
of Muslim-Christian hostilities. Liddle concurred with the implications of these
remarks, noting that while ICMI may not be a threat either to the regime or to
U.S. foreign policy, it "may unleash things,"[23] and thus increase the potential for
domestic instability.

These concerns are echoed by Abdurrahman Wahid, the leader of the traditionalist NU, currently Indonesia's largest Islamic organization, who has been
critical of ICMI for its "sectarian and exclusivist" tendencies. Wahid—who advocates a pluralist interpretation of Islam and democratic politics—has expressed concern that "[ICMI]'s establishment has begun a trend toward the
creation of social organizations and ultimately political parties based on religious and cultural communities."[24] Donald Emmerson of the University of
Wisconsin similarly noted a "disinterring" of certain nationalist traditions
closely associated with the Sukarno era. "I can't help but believe this is being
done, in part, again, to counterbalance the sort of image of the future that ICMI
seems to represent, the 'green image' of the future."[25]

Although these dangers are real, Emmerson further argued that the communal tensions that tore the Indonesian polity apart in the 1950s are not being
replicated today. "The past is not the future of Indonesia."[26] The kind of change
that the society has experienced as a result of the economic changes has radically altered the traditional divisions within Indonesia. Furthermore, the authoritarian nature of the New Order regime will not tolerate such instability.

ISLAM AND MODERNITY

While Indonesia's authoritarian rule makes it difficult to determine precisely
what is happening within the society, the Institute working group did concur
that the country's phenomenal economic growth, coupled with the population
shift associated with the economic changes, has transformed Indonesian society and blurred many of the distinctions within Indonesian Islam. The traditional categories of santri and abangan are gradually disappearing as many
abangan identify with the santri, and as the divisions among the santri lessen.[27]
The development of a more uniform, universalist interpretation of Islam in the
postwar years is contributing to the breakdown of these distinctions, as is the
increasing contact with other Islamic countries and the greater emphasis on religious education.[28]

If the actions of some ICMI activists threaten Indonesia's tolerance for diversity, the development of progressive Islamic thought represents an alternative to this trend. It was argued at the Institute meeting that within Indonesia today there is an effort to redevelop Islam from the inside. This redevelopment is directly linked to economic development and the cultivation of a tolerant modernist thought. "Concurrent with the growth of the Islamic middle class has been a self-conscious attempt on the part of a small group of Islamic intellectuals [the so-called neomodernists] to develop a more open, tolerant, and pluralistic approach to the relationship between state and Islamic society."[29] The resonance of this interpretation of Islam gives some analysts reason to believe that Indonesia may be the "cradle for [the] growth of tolerant Islam."[30]

The modernist dimension of santri Islam has been defined theologically in part by its emphasis on individual interpretation (ijtihad) of the Qur'an. This perspective supports the belief that each generation should reinterpret the teachings of the Qur'an within the context of contemporary situations. The traditionalists, however, have historically placed a greater emphasis on Islamic law and the traditional interpretation of Islam articulated by the Shafi' school of Islamic jurisprudence,[31] with a corresponding deemphasis on ijtihad. The coming together of these two traditions is epitomized by the development of the neomodernist school, a synthesis of the modernist emphasis on ijtihad with the traditionalist appreciation for classical Islamic jurisprudence.

Nurcholish Madjid, a leading spokesman for the neomodernist school, has made several significant contributions to this tolerant interpretation of Islam. These include a strong emphasis on theological substance as opposed to ritual, a rejection of dogmatism (based on the recognition that only God possesses absolute truth), and the belief that there is no single form of government that can be considered uniquely "Islamic."[32] This interpretation of Islam represents a marked divergence from the intolerant form articulated by many Islamic activists or other religious thinkers, and has significantly influenced the leading Islamic intellectuals within ICMI.[33] Scholars such as Liddle see the theological thinking in Indonesia as holding "out more hope than anything else within the Islamic world . . . for the eventual coming to terms of Islam with modernity."[34]

The strength of these ideas is linked to the self-perception or identity of Indonesian Muslims. Particularly within the modernist interpretation, Indonesians have shown a strong desire to be "fully modern people" in terms of having a Western-style education, participating in the international economy, and yet also maintaining their identity as religious people. Indonesia's ability to achieve significant levels of economic growth while maintaining its religious traditions makes it a "spectacular" example for other Islamic countries. Its economic success has helped dispel attitudes that equate Islam with backwardness and, instead, has demonstrated that being Muslim and being modern are not inconsistent. "This is why Indonesia is admired by the Arab intelligentsia."[35]

While the use of Islamic rhetoric—and the elements of intolerance that lurk within ICMI—remains disconcerting for many, others regard the appeal to Islam as perfectly natural. As one participant noted, Muslims in many different countries are seeking to adapt to a rapidly changing international environment. It is only natural that the terms in which they articulate their struggles would be drawn from their own tradition, regardless of whether they are affluent Sunnis seeking to legitimize capitalism or alienated Shi'ites opposing it. "Muslims need to [find] a language within Islam that fits global developments . . . [and helps their societies] adapt to the changing world. And it needs to come from within. . . . Where do they get these values outside of Islam?"[36]

Despite these optimistic assessments of Indonesian Islam, a few words of caution were raised. First, Sidney Jones noted that intellectuals in Indonesia, as in any country, have only limited influence on popular attitudes. Second, despite its support for religious pluralism, the Suharto regime remains politically repressive and authoritarian. While Indonesia may exemplify positive trends, it is "not our kind of society in some fundamental ways."[37] Third, the stability of the situation remains indeterminate. As Dan Brumberg of Georgetown University noted, "the state wants to have its cake and eat it too." The state's efforts to promote a pluralistic Islam is inconsistent with its continued authoritarian rule and the intolerant tendencies of ICMI's social activists. The concern remains that the regime's manipulation of Islam may unleash forces beyond its control.

U.S. POLICY

The overriding concern for U.S. policymakers remains whether or not the positions and activities of the New Order regime are consistent with U.S. foreign policy. United States Institute of Peace Senior Fellow Tahseen Basheer commented that, despite the internal political scene, "I don't see anything in Indonesia that contradicts U.S. interests."[38] The Islamization of Indonesian politics does not appear to be a security risk or major source of concern, apart from the possible internal instability generated by the intercommunal tensions associated with the "greening" of Indonesian politics. On the contrary, as Marvin

Ott of the National Defense University noted, Indonesia's efforts to reconcile Islam with modernity represent a unique opportunity for U.S. policymakers to break out of the traditional framework of analysis, which views Indonesia as either a potential Islamic threat or as a human rights problem, and, instead, appreciate Indonesia as a major force for the modernization of Islam. Such an approach, Ott said, could open the door for a new U.S. role vis-à-vis Islam.

The issues of democratization and human rights, however, do remain problematic. Indonesia's poor human rights record has been regularly criticized by independent human rights groups, the UN Human Rights Commission, and the U.S. Department of State.[39] Although the United States has never sought to sever trade relations on the basis of human rights concerns, the Indonesian regime has seen consistent U.S. congressional concern for human rights—particularly in East Timor—as "anti-Indonesian." As Defense Department analyst Major Dana Dillon noted, from the regime's perspective, it is human rights—and not Islam—that represent the real security threat.[40]

Events in July 1996 indicate that the regime's authoritarian tactics represent a continuing challenge to democratization in the country. The worst rioting in decades broke out in Jakarta in July 1996 after army-backed vigilantes and police stormed the headquarters of the Indonesian Democratic Party (PDI), one of the three official opposition parties. Blame for the resulting violence has been placed on the government and the military. The National Commission on Human Rights, an official group formed by President Suharto, has indicated that it was the government that precipitated the violence and that "the government may have allowed the rioting to rage unchecked as a way of justifying its . . . crackdown on political dissent."[41] Although opposition to the regime remains fragmented, there is a "growing weariness with one-man rule,"[42] something the Suharto regime is aggressively working to counter.

In his summary remarks, Don Emmerson suggested that what Indonesia needs most from the United States is a fairly "hands-off" policy, allowing the current government to evolve into a more pluralist regime through continued economic development and political engagement. Not all would agree with this position,[43] but there may be few alternatives in light of U.S. budgetary constraints. As Emmerson further noted, it will be difficult for the United States to be engaged—or to even have a policy—if it does not have a presence. The "downsizing of U.S. foreign policy"[44] has resulted in the closing of consulates in Indonesia—an action that Indonesians may come to regard as symbolic of diminishing U.S. interest in their country.

Conclusion

The academic and policy debates over Islamic activism are defined by two competing interpretations and, subsequently, two differing prescriptions for U.S. foreign policy. The first interpretation distinguishes between the more extreme or militant activists and the moderate or pragmatic activists. Although extremists are seen to present a problem, most activists are perceived to be moderate and motivated largely by the economic inequity and dysfunctional political systems that exist in their countries. The second interpretation rejects the significance of differentiating moderate from extremist, and sees all activists as inherently hostile to the West and its values. Even though moderate activists may choose less radical tactics, all activists, moderate and extremist alike, are said to share the same ultimate antidemocratic goal.

The Institute series reflected this difference of opinion. At issue was whether a meaningful distinction can, in fact, be made between moderate and extremist Islamic activists, and whether or not pragmatists are capable of accommodation and adjustment within a pluralist system—that is, whether or not they will moderate their views in practice.

The implications of this controversy for policy are significant. If some activists, whatever their ideology, come in practice to reject violence and abide by the rule of law, then, presumably, such behavior ought to be encouraged. Further, if a meaningful distinction can be made between moderates and extremists, then it may be possible to isolate extremists by providing incentives for moderation through greater political participation. If, however, all activists are in essence extremists, then a policy of repression and exclusion would seem justified for *all* activists. The first approach is one of inclusion, the other of exclusion or repression.

The cases examined in this study provide evidence, at least provisionally, that a distinction can be drawn between pragmatists and extremists, and that Islamic activists are divided over the use of political violence and, in some instances, over what they seek. For example, it was suggested that in the case of Iran, leaders are divided between "pragmatists" and "ideologues," even if, at present, the ideologues appear to be in the ascendancy. In the case of Algeria, the Islamic opposition has splintered into numerous factions, with differing views on the use of violent tactics. The dominant groups include the Islamic Salvation Front (the FIS, which is argued to be moderate), the militant Armed Islamic Movement (MIA), and the Armed Islamic Group (GIA). Interestingly, these two militant groups have become rivals and have advocated significantly different policies on such crucial issues as seeking a political settlement with the government.

The divisions among Islamic activists are also illustrated in the case of Jordan and the Palestinians. It was argued in the Institute meeting that both the Muslim Brotherhood in Jordan and Hamas in Gaza and the West Bank have been characterized by social diversity and tensions between the older, more conservative members and the younger, more radical members. The traditional leadership, it was said, had avoided confrontation with the occupying forces, following instead a more gradualist approach, one that emphasized spiritual liberation and the re-creation of Palestinian society through personal conversion. The younger, more radical members sought political liberation through confrontation with Israel, actively opposing the leadership of the traditional conservatives. "The ideological fissures within the Islamic movement centered not on ultimate goals, as both sides wanted the establishment of an Islamic state in all of Palestine with strong ties to the larger Islamic world. Rather, the question was one of tactics: whether it was better to free the soul or the nation first."[1]

These and the other case studies indicate that "Islamic activism" encompasses a broad spectrum of religio-political activists, including militant extremists and pragmatic political operatives, as well as more spiritually oriented figures. Whether this diversity is superficial or whether it attests to a deeper and more lasting division over the basic convictions and objectives of Islamic activism remains open to question. As a result, the implications for policy are not altogether clear. The case studies yield conflicting evidence about the relative merits of the opposing policies of exclusion and inclusion.

For example, the policy of exclusion, or repression, as evidenced in both Algeria and Egypt, does appear largely to have succeeded, if only temporarily, in reducing the militant threats in these two countries. Reports from both places indicate that the militant Islamic groups there are in disarray. Similarly, indications that even moderate activists—in Algeria, for example—are hesitant to embrace democratic norms and genuinely abide by principles of tolerance lend credence to the critique of Islamic activists as antidemocratic, apparently justifying their exclusion from political participation.

Repressive measures, however, have done little to address the underlying economic and political infirmities that plague such countries as Algeria and Egypt. Consequently, the potential for militant extremism remains. Furthermore, the tactics employed by such governments to constrain Islamic activists have in some instances exacerbated discontent by indiscriminately repressing all political opposition, Islamic or secular, moderate or extreme. As a result, the future of democratic development in the region is uncertain, and the possibility that a policy of exclusion is ultimately self-defeating cannot therefore be dismissed.

Similarly, the case studies suggest ambivalent results regarding a policy of inclusion. At first glance, efforts to include, or co-opt, Islamic activists appear to have been successful in moderating Islamic opposition. The best example is in Pakistan, where the participation of the Jama'at-i-Islami within the political process has both mitigated its ideological demands and shaped its largely accommodationist methods. Likewise, in Jordan, it appears that providing even limited political space for the Islamic opposition has successfully minimized extremism and curtailed political violence. Finally, the relatively open political process in Turkey has had a moderating effect on the Islamic Refah party, which has been a fixture in Turkish politics for two decades. Refah's decision to join a coalition government demonstrates its willingness to adjust its ideological goals in response to political pressure.

However, pursuing a policy of inclusion by co-opting the activists or the Islamic message has its price. In Jordan, the Islamic activists remain an obstacle to the Middle East peace process and a continuing force of opposition for the ruling regime; the fact that some activists hold seats in the Jordanian parliament raises the profile and visibility of this opposition. In the case of Pakistan, although the Jama'at has been largely co-opted by the system, it is not clear that Jama'at's participation has invariably contributed to the advance of democracy and tolerance in Pakistan, or that political experience has helped to liberalize its ideals. Rather, the Jama'at's lasting legacy is its politicization of Islam and Islamic issues, which, some would argue, has adversely affected Pakistan society.[2] Controversial Islamic laws were passed during the administration of President Zia-ul-Haq at the behest of the Jama'at that manifest little regard for the rights of minorities or religious dissenters. These efforts have also contributed to the rise of the sectarian parties.

Similarly, in Indonesia, President Suharto's policy of accommodating, if not co-opting, Islam has led to the Islamization or "greening" of political discourse. Although this has allowed a flowering of Islamic modernist thought, there is serious concern that the politicization of religion is increasing communal tensions, eroding the country's tradition of tolerance, and moving Indonesia in an extremist direction. It is not clear, then, that policies of accommodation necessarily produce pluralistic attitudes that foster democratic development. In some cases, accommodation may actually hinder it, raising the question, Who is co-opting whom?

If the policies both of repression and of inclusion have their flaws, is there an alternative? The case studies tend to support the proposal to promote the ideas and institutions of "civil society." This approach emphasizes government accountability, respect for the rule of law, and the development of independent institutions separate from government, including those of the private sector. Civil society is also defined by its tolerance for dissenting views. The cultivation of these institutions and principles is thought to be an effective means of resolving the underlying economic and political problems that, while perhaps not the cause of Islamic extremism, certainly fuel it. A political culture that does not equate dissent with treason or heresy would appear to be critical for addressing both the problems associated with Islamizing political discourse and the need in many countries to ease official restrictions on political dialogue.

Promoting the ideals of civil society also addresses the fundamental dilemma for U.S. policymakers of balancing the long-term goal of democratization with short-term interests in regional stability. Economic, legal, and political reform remain of paramount importance, but reform is gradual and piecemeal, rather than abrupt and systemic. Theoretically, this approach will allow the benefits to be achieved without significant instability and upheaval. In this way, the cornerstones of an open society, such as freedom of the press and of association, can be developed in a manner that will strengthen the moderate center and isolate extremism. As the Indonesian and Turkish cases indicate, the potential for a more tolerant and open interpretation of Islam is greater in societies with higher degrees of economic prosperity and political pluralism.[3]

These case studies further illustrate that Islam, like other religions, can be interpreted in more than one way and that there is possibly no inherent incompatibility between Islam and democracy.[4] Similarly, not all Islamic activists appear, on the surface at least, to be uniformly (or necessarily) antidemocratic. While the ideology, actions, and attitudes of many Islamic activists embody troubling elements of intolerance and frequently advocate discriminatory treatment of minority groups and women, the willingness of many activists to compromise on such issues in practice indicates the adaptability of both the philosophy and the activists. This may reinforce the contention that the problem is not Islam but, rather, extremism and the conditions in which it thrives.

Nonetheless, antidemocratic tendencies remain a significant concern in all of the cases examined, particularly in regard to the Islamization of political discourse. The failure of other political ideologies in the postindependence era allowed Islamic activism to become the dominant voice of opposition throughout the Islamic world. Although it may not have materialized into the monolithic threat that many feared,[5] Islamic activism still remains a "potent ideology of popular dissent"[6] and, as a result, has significantly influenced the language of politics. Islam has become a dominant mode of political discourse by governments and opposition groups throughout the Islamic world.

Although the use of Islamic rhetoric and the lurking elements of intolerance remain disconcerting for many, the appeal of Islam is natural for others. As one participant in the Institute discussion series noted, Muslims in many countries are seeking to adapt to an evolving international environment; it is only natural that the terms in which they articulate their struggle would be drawn from their own tradition. To this end, the development of tolerant interpretations of Islam consistent with the ideals of civil society, such as neomodernist thought in Indonesia, illustrates the positive potential of religion. It also demonstrates that Islam is not synonymous with extremism, and that the real concern for U.S. policymakers is the latter, not the former. "Muslims need to [find] a language within Islam that fits global developments . . . [and helps their societies] adapt to the changing world. And it needs to come from within. . . . Where do they get these values outside of Islam?"[7]

NOTES

SUMMARY

1. These two differing perspectives colored most of the roundtable discussions and reflect both the larger policy debate within Washington and, significantly, the divisions within the different Islamic groups themselves.

2. Others, however, note that the containment policy has been effective in achieving the most basic goal of limiting Iran's export earnings and, consequently, minimizing its ability to support militant groups outside its borders.

3. I. William Zartman, School of Advanced International Studies, Johns Hopkins University (remarks made at the United States Institute of Peace, Washington, D.C., October 14, 1994).

4. William Quandt, University of Virginia (remarks made at the United States Institute of Peace, Washington, D.C., January 5, 1996).

5. Glenn Robinson, Naval Post Graduate School, "Dilemmas of States: Islamicism, Liberalization, and the Arab-Israeli 'End-Game'—The Case of Jordan" (paper presented at the Middle East Studies Association Annual Conference, Phoenix, Arizona, November 1994), 1–2.

6. William Liddle, Ohio State University, "The Islamic Turn in Indonesia: A Political Explanation" (paper presented at the United States Institute of Peace, Washington, D.C., February 2, 1996), 19.

7. Don Emmerson, University of Wisconsin (remarks made at the United States Institute of Peace, Washington, D.C., February 2, 1996).

PREFACE

1. Although Egypt was not considered as a case study, its importance, as well as that of the Muslim Brotherhood, requires comment; for this reason, a brief discussion of Egypt is included in the introductory chapter. Another important case, Saudi Arabia, was not included in this project because of the need to limit the number of case studies. Because of its Wahhabi tradition and the country's strategic importance to the

United States, Saudi Arabia is, however, a case study worth pursuing in any further discussion of Islamic activism and U.S. foreign policy.

INTRODUCTION

1. We have chosen to use the term "Islamic activism" in preference to other familiar terms. We take it to refer to Muslims who *actively seek social and political transformation in keeping with a particular interpretation of Islamic teaching.* Although alternative descriptions of the same phenomenon will continue to be used, they have various disadvantages. "Islamic fundamentalism" is frequently applied or interpreted in a pejorative way, and its use therefore tends to impede rather than facilitate dialogue and discussion. Similarly, terms like "Islamism" and "political Islam" run the risk of implying that there exists one consistent and unified political ideology that unites all members of the various Islamic movements. That assumption, however, is open to question. While some tenets are held in common, other beliefs about such things as the permissibility of using violence or the compatibility between modern democracy and Islamic ideals are, apparently, a matter of serious disagreement among activists. It seems judicious, therefore, to select a term that is sufficiently neutral and open-ended that it does not beg questions as to whether the phenomenon under consideration is one thing or many. Finally, "Islamicists" can be confusing since this term is used to describe both politically active Muslims and scholars of Islam. Throughout the report, the words "fundamentalism" and "Islamism" occasionally appear in the quoted statements of participants or scholarly writings. These terms are considered to be synonyms for "Islamic activism."

2. The arguments attributed to this position were articulated in a paper delivered by Martin Kramer, "The Mismeasure of Political Islam," at Georgetown University, Washington, D.C., on April 11, 1995.

3. According to this perspective, activists (moderate or extremist) are defined by their "religious intolerance; a rejection of social, political or legal equality for women; a repudiation of the belief in the sovereignty of man or the right of a citizenry to choose its leaders . . . ; and avowed opposition to coexistence with legitimate governments of Muslim-majority states that refuse to accept Islamist dogma." Robert Satloff, Washington Institute for Near East Policy, in correspondence.

4. Daniel Pipes cited in "Symposium: Resurgent Islam in the Middle East," *Middle East Policy* 3, no. 2 (August 1994): 6.

5. Kramer, "The Mismeasure of Political Islam."

6. Jordan was cited as an example of this phenomenon.

7. Lisa Anderson, Columbia University (remarks made at the United States Institute of Peace symposium, "Political Islam in the Middle East: Its Regional and International Implications," Washington, D.C., March 2, 1994).

8. Both the Clinton and the Bush administrations have explicitly rejected the notion that Islamic activism is a monolithic entity. Public perceptions, however, are not as nuanced. See the section in this chapter on "Policy Implications."

9. William Quandt, University of Virginia (remarks made at the United States Institute of Peace, Washington, D.C., January 5, 1996).

10. Anthony Lake (remarks presented at the Washington Institute for Near East Policy, Washington, D.C., May 17, 1994).

11. "Islamic revivalism and Islamic movements are integral to Islamic history and in some sense may be seen as part of a recurrent revivalist cycle in history, [though] most movements today differ from those of earlier centuries in that they are modern, not traditional, in their leadership, ideology, and organization." John Esposito, *The Islamic Threat: Myth or Reality?* (New York: Oxford University Press, 1992), 119—120.

12. Ibid., 50.

13. Mumtaz Ahmad, "Islamic Fundamentalism in South Asia," in *Fundamentalisms Observed,* ed. Martin E. Marty and R. Scott Appleby (Chicago: University of Chicago Press, 1991), 460.

14. Ibid., 461.

15. Ibid.

16. Albert Hourani, *A History of the Arab Peoples* (New York: Warner Books, 1991), 343.

17. Majid Khadduri, *Political Trends in the Arab World* (Baltimore: Johns Hopkins Press, 1970), 23-24.

18. The failure of Arab state politics significantly shaped the ideology and methods of the Muslim Brotherhood in Egypt, which has in turn influenced Islamic activism throughout the Islamic world. This section does not assume that all Arabs are Muslim nor that all Muslims are Arab. Rather, it highlights this period of history in recognition of the influence it had on the development of Islamic activism. Furthermore, the focus on the region is particularly helpful in understanding the militancy of Islamic activism, since the activist movements in Pakistan, Malaysia, and other non-Arab countries (with the exception of Iran) have not been as violent or rejectionist as have been many of the groups in the Middle East and North Africa.

19. The Islamic movements that developed in the preindependence era opposed the secularizing tendency of the socialist parties. In Egypt, for example, despite concessions to the Islamic agenda, the Nasser regime did not establish an Islamic constitution or impose *shari'a* law. Consequently, the Islamic activists opposed the regime and became the target of state repression.

20. Robert Oakley, National Defense University, in correspondence.

21. Muhammad Faour, *The Arab World after Desert Storm* (Washington, D.C.: United States Institute of Peace Press, 1993), 55.

22. Hourani, *A History of the Arab Peoples,* 452.

23. While Islamic activists advocate a return to Islam, "they do not seek to reproduce the past but to reconstruct society through a process of Islamic reform in which the principles and values of Islam are applied to contemporary needs." John Esposito, in testimony before the House Committee on Foreign Affairs, *Islamic Fundamentalism* *in Africa and Implications for U.S. Policy: A Hearing before the Subcommittee on Africa,* 102d Cong., 2d sess., May 20, 1992, 31.

24. Ahmad, "Islamic Fundamentalism in South Asia," 463.

25. Graham Fuller, in his July 1994 presentation to the Institute roundtable, noted that countries exhibiting certain characteristics will be vulnerable to Islamic extremism. These characteristics include:

1. Adverse economic and social conditions.

2. Political repression and the loss of legitimacy such repression causes.

3. The absence of a viable political opposition, providing a vacuum that is readily filled by religious movements.

4. The existence of an outside, non-Muslim threat (real or imagined).

5. A sense of humiliation born of the colonial experience, and the related and current sense of victimhood that results from the existing "gross imbalance of power."

6. A craving for a sense of dignity and authenticity absent from many countries since the end of colonialism.

26. Esposito, *Islamic Threat,* 74.

27. It is difficult to ascribe motives. While religion is manipulated for political ends throughout the world, many political activists—Islamic, Jewish, Christian, or Hindu—appear sincerely to believe their actions are in accord with religious principles, and say that they are reacting to an onslaught on traditional values by secular (and hence profane) society. Indeed, it is difficult to understand their actions outside of a religious context. Other activists, however, are more opportunistic and appeal to religion because it is an effective way to mobilize political support.

28. Charles B. Strozier, "Religious Militancy or 'Fundamentalism,'" in *Religion and Human Rights,* ed. John Kelsay and Sumner B. Twiss (New York: Project on Religion and Human Rights, 1994), 23.

29. Dirk Vandewalle, Dartmouth College (remarks made at the United States Institute of Peace symposium, "Political Islam in the Middle East: Its Regional and International Implications," Washington, D.C., March 2, 1994).

30. Alan Richards, "Islam or Economics: A Perspective on the True Causes of Instability" (paper presented at the Center for Strategic and International Studies, Washington, D.C., September 7, 1995).

31. Faour, *The Arab World after Desert Storm,* 31.

32. Anderson, *Political Islam in the Middle East,* 26. This point is reiterated by Mohammed Faour: "Arab democracy seems to be largely a new face on an old system of authoritarianism. . . . The Gulf War may have increased popular demands for democracy and elicited from reluctant Arab regimes some prodemocratic rhetoric, but it has not significantly reduced the obstacles to democratic development." Faour, *The Arab World after Desert Storm,* 33.

33. Satloff, in correspondence.

34. "An Islamic state cannot be isolated from society because Islam is a comprehensive, integrated way of life. The division between private and public, the state and society . . . has not been known in Islam. The state is only the political expression of an Islamic society." Hasan al-Turabi, "The Islamic State," in *Voices of Resurgent Islam*, ed. John L. Esposito (New York: Oxford University Press, 1983), 241.

35. U.S. Department of State, *Country Reports for 1993* (Washington, D.C.: U.S. Government Printing Office, 1994), 284.

36. According to the proponents of Islamic activism, the Western model encourages social fragmentation. Political, economic, and ethnic groups, driven by nothing more than their own self-interest, compete divisively with one another. There is no common unifying value system, a problem exacerbated by the fact that religion is sharply distinguished from government and law, as well as from the economy and other aspects of society. By contrast, the activists assert that Islam provides an integrated way of life and an encompassing worldview.

37. Francis Deng, "Tragedy in Sudan: A Personal Appeal to Compatriots and to Humanity," *Mediterranean Quarterly* (winter 1994): 47.

38. U.S. State Department, *Country Reports for 1993*, 279.

39. Charles Adams, "Mawdudi and the Islamic State," in Voices of Resurgent Islam, ed. Esposito, 111.

39. On the contrary, according to Nurcholish Majdid, a leading spokesman for the neomodernist school, "many forms of government, including that based on *Pancasila*, are in accordance with God's will." (*Pancasila*, literally meaning "five principles," served as the ideological basis for the Indonesian government under Presidents Sukarno and Suharto.) William Liddle, Ohio State University, "The Islamic Turn in Indonesia: A Political Explanation" (paper presented at the United States Institute of Peace, Washington, D.C., February 2, 1996), 19.

41. Although the use of force in the pursuit of religious and political reform is not uncommon in Islamic history (similar to all other religious traditions), Islam does not condone the indiscriminate use of violence. Scholars note that Islamic teachings have been actively concerned to limit the occurrence and conduct of war in very specific ways. At an early stage of its development, Islam contained plentiful examples of injunctions against killing women, children, and other noncombatants. At the same time, there are certain justifications—particularly appealing to the extremists or militants—for relaxing such restrictions under what are believed to be emergency conditions. These two interpretations reflect a deep division among activists over the proper use of violence in achieving political goals. See John Kelsay, *Islam and War: A Study in Comparative Ethics* (Louisville: Westminster, 1993), 53.

42. John Voll, "Fundamentalism in the Sunni Arab World: Egypt and the Sudan," in *Fundamentalisms Observed*, ed. Marty and Appleby, 383.

43. Ibid.

44. Kelsay, *Islam and War*, 99–106.

45. "[W]ith regard to the lands of Islam, the enemy lives right in the middle of them. The enemy even has got hold of the reins of power, for this enemy is (none other than) those rulers who have (illegally) seized the leadership of the Muslims. Therefore, waging jihad against them is an individual duty, in addition to the fact that Islamic jihad today requires a drop of sweat from every Muslim." From *The Neglected Duty,* cited in Kelsay, *Islam and War,* 106.

46. See Kelsay, *Islam and War,* 104. Under the international laws of war, "military necessity" is not unrestricted. Presumably, therefore, anyone invoking the idea is bound by its limitations. "Military necessity" is "the principle which justifies measures of regulated force *not [otherwise] forbidden by international law* which are indispensable for securing the prompt submission of the enemy, with least possible expenditures of economic and human resources." Cited in William V. O'Brien, "International Law and the Western Just War Tradition," in *Just War and Jihad,* ed. John Kelsay and James Turner Johnson (New York: Greenwood Press, 1991), 166 (emphasis added).

47. Kelsay, *Islam and War,* 107.

48. "*Jus in bello* requirements like [noncombatant] discrimination and proportionality are not overridden in the Hamas Charter or *The Neglected Duty,* but the peculiar type of conflict in which Hamas or Islamic Jihad find themselves involved creates situations in which traditional applications of these notions must be stretched." Kelsay, *Islam and War,* 107.

49. As one Muslim Brother leader, Umar al-Tilmisani, noted, "reliance upon weapons results in destruction. The Brethren do not consider revolution, nor do they depend upon it, nor do they believe in its utility or its outcome." Referenced by Sana Abed-Kotob in "The Accommodationists Speak: Goals and Strategies of the Muslim Brotherhood of Egypt," *International Journal of Middle East Studies* 27 (1995): 324.

50. Yusuf al-Qaradawi, *Islamic Awakening: Between Rejection and Extremism,* 2d ed. (Herndon, Virginia: American Trust Publication and the International Institute of Islamic Thought, 1991), 39.

51. Hasan al-Banna, "The New Renaissance," in *Islam in Transition: Muslim Perspectives,* ed. John J. Donohue and John L. Esposito (New York: Oxford University Press, 1982), 82.

52. Al-Qaradawi, *Islamic Awakening,* 46. A specific reference is made to the Prophet Mohammed's rebuke of a man who had killed another Muslim. The rebuked man claimed that the dead one's allegiance to Islam was not sincere. The Prophet rejected this excuse by questioning the ability of any person to know the depth of another's faith: "Did you look into his heart after he had confessed that there is no God but Allah?"

53. Jad-ul-Haq Ali Jad-ul-Haq.

54. Kelsay, *Islam and War,* 105—106.

55. Ibid., 105.

56. Ibid.

57. Suggested in comments from Robert Satloff (United States Institute of Peace meeting, Washington, D.C., January 5, 1996), although the typology worked out here differs from the one he proposed.

58. Anthony Lake (remarks presented at the Washington Institute for Near East Policy, Washington, D.C., May 17, 1994).

59. Robert Pelletreau, cited in cited in "Symposium: Resurgent Islam in the Middle East," *Middle East Policy* 3, no. 2 (August 1994): 3.

60. Reuters News Service, "Strategy in Algeria," *Washington Post,* October 10, 1995.

61. Judith Miller, "The Challenge of Radical Islam," *Foreign Affairs* 72, no. 2 (spring 1993): 53; and "Islam and the West," *Economist,* August 6, 1994.

62. The overt support of Iraq by the United States until shortly before the invasion of Kuwait, even when Iraq was using chemical weapons on its Kurdish minorities, has similarly brought into question U.S. impartiality and dedication to human rights standards.

63. If some critics feel U.S. policy overlooks the faults of regional allies, others believe that the U.S. government does not provide enough support for such allies. These latter critics argue that the United States should be more active in opposing Islamic activism, and that the United States should overtly support "those governments and groups in combat with the Fundamentalists." Daniel Pipes, cited in "Symposium: Resurgent Islam in the Middle East," *Middle East Policy* 3, no. 2 (August 1994): 7.

64. The electoral strength of such groups is based on their relatively strong organizations in states where formal opposition is banned and where few, if any, alternatives to the existing government exist. Coupled with the lack of popularity of many regimes, the stage is set for a rejectionist vote, the beneficiaries of which are the Islamic activists. Miller, "Challenge of Radical Islam," 52.

65. Edward Djerejian, address at Meridian House, Washington, D.C., June 2, 1992; reprinted in *Middle East Policy* 1, no. 4 (1992): 160.

66. Phebe Marr, "The U.S., Europe, and the Middle East: An Uneasy Triangle," *Middle East Journal* 48, no. 2 (spring 1994): 213.

67. Lally Weymouth, "Mubarak's Battle Gets Personal," *Washington Post,* July 14, 1995.

68. John Lancaster, "Praised Abroad, Egypt's Ruler Faltering at Home," *Washington Post,* March 13, 1995.

69. In the case of Egypt, for example, the U.S. policy approach reflects that country's key contribution to the Middle East peace process.

70. Robert Oakley, National Defense University (remarks made at the United States Institute of Peace, Washington, D.C., February 2, 1996).

71. Earlier, in the 1977 elections, Islamic issues were politicized to such an extent that the socialist prime minister, Zulifikar Ali Bhutto, was forced to put forward Islamic reforms in the postelection period.

72. Miller, "Challenge of Radical Islam," 53.

73. John Esposito, cited in "Symposium: Resurgent Islam in the Middle East," *Middle East Policy* 3, no. 2 (August 1994): 6.

74. Particularly relevant here are the concepts of individual rights and public space. Rami Khouri, *Jordan Times,* as reported in the *MidEast Mirror,* September 26, 1995, 15.

75. Augustus Richard Norton, "The Future of Civil Society in the Middle East," *Middle East Journal,* 47, no. 2 (spring 1993): 214.

76. To this end, the distinction between pragmatist and extremist becomes meaningful.

1. IRAN

1. Shaul Bakhash, George Mason University, "Islam, Ideology, and Foreign Policy in Iran" (paper presented at the United States Institute of Peace, Washington, D.C., September 30, 1994), 2.

2. Bakhash, "Islam, Ideology, and Foreign Policy in Iran," 9. Other participants, however, noted that Iran's public statements at the time condemned the United States and that Iran continues to oppose the U.S. military presence in the Persian Gulf.

3. Bakhash, workshop discussion.

4. Martin Kramer, Georgetown University, workshop discussion.

5. Thomas Friedman, "Wednesday News Quiz," *New York Times,* March 29, 1995.

6. The embargo has adversely affected Iranian oil revenues and initially sparked a currency crisis that hurt Iran's foreign exchange earnings. It has also affected Iran's ability to raise money abroad. While in the short run, the embargo has achieved its intended effect, it is not clear that in the long run it will be successful, as non-U.S. companies move to invest in new oil and gas projects within Iran.

7. The legislation, originally introduced by U.S. Senator Alfonse D'Amato (R-NY) as S. 1228, contains punitive measures against firms in violation of the law. These sanctions include denial of Export-Import Bank assistance, prohibition on loans or credits from U.S. financial institutions, and potential denial of U.S. government procurement opportunities. Similar legislation, H.R. 2172, was introduced in the U.S. House of Representatives by Representatives Gilman, Berman, King, and Lantos.

8. "Our goal is to convince the leadership in Tehran to abandon [policies inconsistent with international law] and to abide by international norms." The Honorable Peter Tarnoff, Under Secretary of State for Political Affairs, Department of State, in testimony before the House Committee on International Relations, *U.S. Policy toward Iran: Hearing before the Committee on International Relations,* 104th Cong., 1st sess., November 9, 1995, 47.

9. John Diamond, "Replacing Iran Regime Advocated by Gingrich," *Washington Post,* February 9, 1995.

10. William Quandt, University of Virginia (remarks made at the United States Institute of Peace, Washington, D.C., January 5, 1995).

11. Bernard Lewis, Princeton University, workshop discussion.

12. Andrew Whitley, Clark and Weinstock, Inc., workshop discussion.

13. The basis of this approach was to create an external environment that strengthened the pragmatists by exacting a price for Iranian radicalism. Peter Rodman, Center for Strategic and International Studies, workshop discussion.

14. Bakhash and Ellen Laipson both noted that there was an opening after the Gulf War for some form of rapprochement, though this opening was short-lived, since the

U.S. response did not meet Iranian expectations. Iran is still seeking financial claims from the United States, as well as an apology for the accidental downing of an Iranian airliner over the Persian Gulf by a U.S. warship. Aziz Sachedina, however, questioned the Iranian commitment to a rapprochement at that time, noting that the regime's rhetoric within the country did not change, despite an apparent shift in rhetoric produced for foreign observers. Bakhash; Ellen Laipson, National Security Council; Aziz Sachedina, University of Virginia: contributions to workshop discussion.

15. Bruce Riedel, Deputy Assistant Secretary of Defense for Near Eastern and South Asian Affairs, in testimony before the House Committee on International Relations, *U.S. Policy toward Iran: Hearing before the Committee on International Relations,* 104th Cong., 1st sess., November 9, 1995, 47.

16. In 1992, the Chinese agreed to provide Iran with two light-water power reactors. China, however, has yet to provide Iran with these reactors.

17. Thomas Lippman, "Stepped up Nuclear Effort Renews Alarm about Iran," *Washington Post,* April 17, 1995.

18. R. Jeffrey Smith, "China Nuclear Deal with Iran Is Feared," *Washington Post,* April 17, 1995.

19. Shaul Bakhash, "Iran's 'Islamic' Foreign Policy" (paper presented at the United States Institute of Peace, Washington, D.C., May 1994), 18.

20. In a speech delivered in March 1996, Palestinian National Authority Chairman Yasir Arafat accused Iran of being behind the February 1996 bombings in Israel. The Iranian government denied these accusations. "Iran Denies Involvement in Israel Bomb Attacks," *Washington Post,* March 8, 1996.

21. Iran has directly supported Shi'i factions in Afghanistan and Pakistan that are opposed to Sunni groups supported by Saudi Arabia. This is part of a competition over Islamic leadership between Iran and Saudi Arabia. Robert Oakley in correspondence.

22. Edward G. Shirley, "The Iran Policy Trap," *Foreign Policy* 96 (fall 1994): 81.

23. Bakhash, "Iran's 'Islamic' Foreign Policy," 10.

24. Ibid., 5.

25. Ibid., 6.

26. Ibid.

27. Masood Ghaznavi, Rosemont College, workshop discussion.

28. Sachedina, workshop discussion.

2. ALGERIA

1. William Zartman, Johns Hopkins University, School of Advanced International Studies (remarks made at the United States Institute of Peace, Washington, D.C., November 14, 1994).

2. Dirk Vandewalle, "At the Brink: Chaos in Algeria," *World Policy Journal* 9, no. 4 (fall–winter 1992): 709.

3. It was under these reforms that the FIS was established as a political party.

4. Mona Yacoubian, Council on Foreign Relations, in correspondence.

5. John Entelis and Lisa Arone, "Algeria in Turmoil: Islam, Democracy, and the State," *Middle East Policy* I, no. 2 (1992): 23.

6. Ibid., 29.

7. William Zartman, in testimony before the House Committee on Foreign Affairs, *The Crisis in Algeria: Hearing before the Committee on Foreign Affairs*, 103rd Cong., 2d sess., March 22, 1994, 2.

8. Robin Wright, *Los Angeles Times*, workshop discussion. Remark based on personal interviews conducted in Algeria prior to the December 1991 legislative elections.

9. Wright, workshop discussion.

10. Yacoubian, in correspondence.

11. Amnesty International, *Algeria: Repression and Violence Must End* (Washington, D.C.: Amnesty International, October 1994), ii.

12. This point is meant to illustrate that, contrary to popular opinion, the 1992 elections did not reflect support for the FIS, but, rather, "that the majority of the population in Algeria rejected the two major alternatives and the pale third option (third parties) offered to it. . . . The elections show that all three options in Algeria are incapable of attracting solid popular support, and incapable of offering a solid program." Zartman in testimony before House Foreign Affairs Committee, *Crisis in Algeria,* 2.

13. Wright, workshop discussion.

14. Ibid.

15. Robin Wright, "A Fight for Democracy in the Middle East: 'The Battle of Algiers' Part II," *Los Angeles Times*, January I, 1995.

16. Zartman, workshop discussion. Gowher Rizvi argued that there is nothing inherently anti-Western about the position of the Islamic activists. He noted that the struggle within Algeria is an internal dispute rooted in economic and political issues. Anti-Western sentiment is created, however, when the population sees Western support for corrupt regimes, such as the support for the FLN. "[Western governments] end up supporting very repressive regimes . . . because they are supposedly modernist and in the process [they] alienate many" who would not otherwise have supported the Islamists. Gowher Rizvi, Asia Society, workshop discussion.

17. Specific references are attributed to Ali Belahadj, of the FIS leadership. Gehad Auda, Center for Strategic and International Studies, workshop discussion. Zartman in testimony before House Foreign Affairs Committee, *Crisis in Algeria,* 4.

18. Abdullahi An-Na'im remarked that the emphasis on apostasy and heresy in the Sudanese interpretation of *shari'a* has been used as a pretext for violently suppressing dissent within the political community, and that "*shari'a* as an ideology is undemocratic." Abdullahi An-Na'im, Human Rights Watch/Africa, workshop discussion.

19. This issue remains a continuing source of debate within policy and academic circles. See Timothy D. Sisk, *Islam and Democracy: Religion, Politics, and Power in the Middle East* (Washington, D.C.: United States Institute of Peace Press, 1992).

20. The reforms would promote free-market economics, shorter the presidential term, and create a supreme court and senate. It would also prohibit political parties from making explicit displays of religious and ethnic militancy. "In Bid to Restore Order, Algeria Proposes Reforms," *New York Times,* May 13, 1996.

21. Official estimates place the turnout at 75 percent of the nearly 16 million Algerian voters.

22. "Algeria: Time to Talk Turkey," *MidEast Mirror,* November 24, 1995.

23. The stamina of the regime is due in part to a deep resolve within the Algerian elite and the military to maintain the existing order; many among this group fear that if the reins of power were relinquished, they would lose everything. Martin Kramer, Georgetown University, workshop discussion.

24. The FIS, in public statements, has committed itself to a negotiated solution.

25. Qusai Saleh Darwish in *Asharq al-Awsat,* "No Room for Optimism about the New Round of Political Talks in Algeria," as reported in *MidEast Mirror,* March 29, 1995, 19.

26. To many in the workshop, continuation of the current situation was seen to be untenable and represented a worst-case scenario.

27. "Algerian Opposition Repeats Call for a 'Return to Politics,'" *MidEast Mirror,* March 23, 1995, 15.

28. "Platform for a Peaceful Political Solution to Algeria's Crisis," *MidEast Mirror,* January 16, 1995, 24.

29. The regime's stated reason for rejecting the document was that it was constructed outside of Algeria, and that the issues addressed in the platform should be the topic of discussion within the country.

30. Lally Weymouth, "A Deal with Terror," *Washington Post,* April 11, 1995.

31. Ibid.

32. Ibid.

33. Chris Hedges, "France Wages a Lonely Battle with Radical Islam," *New York Times,* January 1, 1995.

34. "The United States has agreed, at French urging, to support the Paris Club rescheduling of over $5 billion in Algerian official debt." Peter Rodman, "The Time Bomb in Algeria," *Washington Post,* January 1, 1995.

35. U.S. policy has sought to avoid both "the emergence of a fanatical regime in Algeria [or] the descent of this important state into chaos." Statement by C. David Welch, principal deputy assistant secretary of state for Near Eastern Affairs, before the House Committee on International Relations, *Terrorism in Algeria: Hearing before the Subcommittee on Africa of the Committee on International Relations,* 104th Cong., 1st sess., October 11, 1995, 24.

36. Andrew J. Pierre and William B. Quandt, *The Algerian Crisis: Policy Options for the West* (Washington, D.C.: Carnegie Endowment for International Peace, 1996), 52.

37. Mona Yacoubian Council on Foreign Relations, (remarks made at United States Institute of Peace meeting, Washington, D.C., January 5, 1995).

38. Pierre and Quandt, *Algerian Crisis,* 53.

39. Assistant Secretary Pelletrau recently visited Algeria and met with President Zeroual.

40. William Quandt (remarks made at United States Institute of Peace meeting, Washington, D.C., January 5, 1995), 15.

41. Jim Hoagland, "A Defining Moment in Algeria—for Us," *Washington Post,* September 22, 1994.

42. Daniel Brumberg, Georgetown University, workshop discussion.

3. JORDAN AND THE PALESTINIANS

1. Glenn Robinson, Naval Post Graduate School, workshop discussion.

2. The Hashemite monarchy traces its lineage to the Prophet Mohammed's clan, and has been known as the guardians of the holy sites in Jerusalem.

3. It was argued that while there have been areas of overlapping interests, the periodic repression and imprisonment of the Brotherhood's leadership precludes the conclusion that there has been active support by the Brotherhood for the Hashemite regime.

4. Robert Satloff, *"They Cannot Stop our Tongues": Islamic Activism in Jordan* (Washington, D.C.: Washington Institute for Near East Policy, 1986), 3.

5. Robert Satloff, "Jordan's Great Gamble," in *The Politics of Economic Reform in the Middle East,* ed. Henri J. Barkey (London: St. Martin's Press, 1992), 144–145.

6. Robinson, workshop discussion.

7. The Muslim Brotherhood was legalized in the 1940s; it retained this status even under martial law in 1967.

8. Robinson, workshop discussion.

9. Robert Satloff (remarks made at the United States Institute of Peace symposium, "Political Islam in the Middle East: Its Regional and International Implications," Washington, D.C., March 2, 1994). The reference refers to a comment made by a Jordanian intelligence officer.

10. Glenn Robinson, "To Free the Soul or Free the Nation? The Islamicist Movement in the West Bank and Gaza Strip" (background paper to workshop at the United States Institute of Peace, December 14, 1994), 2.

11. Satloff, *Political Islam in the Middle East,* 136.

12. Satloff, "Jordan's Great Gamble," 133.

13. Robinson, "To Free the Soul or Free the Nation?" 16.

14. Jean François Legrain: "Hamas: Legitimate Heir of Palestinian Nationalism?" (paper presented at the United States Institute of Peace symposium, "Political Islam in the Middle East: Its Regional and International Implications," Washington, D.C., March 2, 1994).

15. The active confrontation of the Intifada undermined the PLO "policy which, since the beginning of the seventies, restricted itself to manage a 'normalized' occupation inside the territories." Ibid.

16. The term *hamas* has been alternately translated as "zeal," "strength," and "bravery."

17. According to Hamas, "Zionism and Israeli occupation, in respect to re-Islamization, [is] an obstacle which cannot be bypassed; therefore, their destruction becomes an immediate and individual Islamic duty." Legrain, "Hamas," 2.

18. "[T]here is no possibility of recognizing Israel or coexisting with it or accepting it in the Islamic movement." Interview with Mahmoud Zahhar, spokesman of the Palestinian Islamic Resistance Movement (Hamas) by the newspaper *al-Hayat*; see *Mideast Mirror*, December 16, 1994, 11.

19. Clyde Mark and Kenneth Katzman, *Hamas and the Palestinian Islamic Jihad: Recent Developments* (Washington, D.C.: Congressional Research Service, December 12, 1994), 3.

20. As the neighbor of a suicide bomber affiliated with Islamic Jihad said, "Anwar [the bomber] did to the Israelis what they are doing to us." "Suicide Bombs Kill 19 in Israel: Shadow Cast over Peace Talks," *New York Times*, January 23, 1995.

21. This discussion comes from Rami G. Khouri of the *Jordan Times*; see *Mideast Mirror*, January 24, 1995, 9.

22. Chris Hedges, "A Language Divided against Itself," *New York Times*, January 28, 1995.

23. Martin Kramer, Georgetown University, workshop discussion.

24. The link between violence and negotiations is not uncommon. The negotiations over the future South Africa were marred by continuing violence, even into the later stages leading up to the national elections. The logic behind such acts is the desire to gain tactical advantages by threatening the whole process. The closer a settlement comes to resolution, the more likely that marginalized groups will resort to violence. Militancy remains the last recourse for those who stand to lose from a change in the status quo—the so-called enemies of peace—whether they are Jewish, Muslim, or Christian. See Tim Sisk, *Democratization in South Africa: The Elusive Social Contract* (Princeton: Princeton University Press, 1994).

25. "Arab commentators Monday justify the Islamic Jihad suicide attack that killed 19 Israelis—18 of them soldiers—and wounded 64 at Beit Lid junction near Netanya on Sunday, with one columnist in Bahrain describing it as 'fresh glad tidings.'" *Mideast Mirror*, January 23, 1995, 8.

26. At the same time, there are signs in the opposite direction. The attendance of a number of Arab heads of state at the funeral of Prime Minister Yitzhak Rabin gave an intangible boost to the peace process. The image of Arab leaders mourning the death of an Israeli prime minister demonstrated a change in attitude toward Israel among its neighbors. The Sharm al-Sheikh conference in March 1996 demonstrated a similar sense of support among Arab states for the peace process.

27. The majority of its activities are not military. "The military commando wing of Hamas . . . numbers [only] around 100 members at any given time." Mark and Katzman, *Hamas and the Palestinian Islamic Jihad*, 3.

28. Legrain, "Hamas," 5.

29. Mark and Katzman, *Hamas and the Palestinian Islamic Jihad,* 6.

30. Covenant of the Islamic Resistance, Article 1, 4.

31. For example, the organization's rejection of the Peace Accords is premised on a religious claim that Palestine is an Islamic land, which is inseparable from the whole of the Muslim world and which no temporal authority can divide. Robinson, "To Free the Soul or Free the Nation?" 22. See also Hamas Covenant, Article 11, 9.

32. "The liberation of Palestine is . . . an individual duty for every Moslem wherever he may be. On this basis the problem should be viewed. This should be realized by every Moslem." Hamas Covenant, Article 14, 13.

33. "The Islamic Resistance Movement emerged to carry out its role through striving for the sake of its Creator, its arms intertwined with those of all the fighters for the liberation of Palestine." Hamas Covenant, Introduction, 2–3.

34. Robinson, "To Free the Soul or Free the Nation?" 35.

35. *Mideast Mirror,* December 1, 1995, 12.

36. Jean François Legrain (remarks at the United States Institute of Peace symposium, "Political Islam in the Middle East: Its Regional and International Implications," Washington, D.C., March 2, 1994).

37. Some observers believe Hamas received support from Israel prior to 1987 in an effort to offset and undermine PLO influence in the occupied territories. This view is disputed, however, by others who argue that Hamas was given little attention—one way or another—by Israel until the Islamists became violent.

38. "Even as the parameters of their political discourse narrowed, the relationship on the street between Hamas and Fatah activists was often hostile." Robinson, "To Free the Soul or Free the Nation?" 36.

39. *Mideast Mirror,* December 1, 1995, 11.

40. Kramer, workshop discussion.

41. Interview with Zahhar, Hamas spokesman, in *Mideast Mirror,* December 16, 1994, 11.

42. "If there are significant changes on the ground within the West Bank as a result of Israeli policies, then the despair [and cynicism] on the part of a great deal of the population [would dissipate, and support for Hamas would diminish]." Graham Fuller, RAND Corporation, luncheon discussion.

43. While most polls place support for Hamas at between 12 and 17 percent (as opposed to 40 to 42 percent for Fatah), the Israeli Army estimates that more than 40 to 50 percent of the Palestinian population in Gaza and the West Bank support Hamas activities. (Legrain, *Political Islam in the Middle East,* 7.) These data reflect the division between the "soft" and "hard" support for Hamas.

44. Mark and Katzman, *Hamas and the Palestinian Islamic Jihad,* 6.

45. Robinson, luncheon discussion. The South African agreement made it clear up front that the end product of negotiations would be a multiracial democratic state. How this was to be achieved was the subject of the subsequent negotiations.

46. "[The statement] transforms the nature of the conflict from a struggle against occupation, racism, displacement, economic exploitation, and the future of a national liberation movement to rendering the Palestinians as foreigners in their own land. The powers given to the administrative council are limited. It has [put] Palestinians on reservations with no real authority over land, water, and other resources. . . . It is seen as a deception, because it is a redeployment of Israeli forces, not a withdrawal. . . . The settlements have not stopped. . . . What we have is a new world order in which the Arab world is still being redivided into many, many little things." Yvonne Haddad (remarks made at the United States Institute of Peace symposium, "Political Islam in the Middle East: Its Regional and International Implications," Washington, D.C., March 2, 1994).

47. Yossi Melman, "War and Peace Process," *Washington Post,* January 28, 1995.

48. Margaret Carpenter, assistant administrator of the U.S. Agency for International Development; see *Mideast Mirror,* July 14, 1995, 4.

49. Barton Gellman, "Israeli First: Word 'Torture' Is Spoken," *Washington Post,* October 21, 1995. The necessity defense is the argument that a breach of law (in this instance, the 1984 UN Convention against Torture) is necessary to avert a greater harm, such as a terrorist attack.

50. It should be noted that before the signing of the Oslo Accords, such structures were either limited or specifically precluded under Israeli occupation.

51. "While it is premature to speak of any pattern of systematic abuses, the PA has not demonstrated a commitment to installing the rule of law. It is responsible for a series of arbitrary and repressive measures while at the same time failing to make clear what laws and regulations are in effect and to show any commitment to investigating and punishing human rights violations." "The Gaza Strip and Jericho: Human Rights under Palestinian Partial Self-Rule," *Human Rights Watch/Middle East* 7, no. 2 (February 1995): 14.

52. "In order to make peace with Israel, Arab regimes have had to, and will continue to have to, contain the Islamist opposition," Glenn Robinson, "Dilemmas of States: Islamicism, Liberalization, and the Arab-Israeli 'End-Game'—The Case of Jordan" (paper presented at the Middle East Studies Association Annual Conference, Phoenix, Arizona, November 1994), 1.

53. Ibid., 1–2.

54. Satloff, *Islamic Activism in Jordan,* v.

55. Serge Schmemann, "In Jordan, Bread-Price Protests Signal Deep Anger," *New York Times,* August 21, 1996.

56. President Clinton in remarks to the Jordanian Parliament, Amman, Jordan, October 26, 1994.

57. Anthony Lake (remarks presented at the Washington Institute for Near East Policy, Washington, D.C., May 17, 1994).

58. David D. Newsom, "End a No-Result Policy in Israel," *Christian Science Monitor,* September 27, 1996.

59. Robinson, in correspondence.

60. Kramer, workshop discussion.

61. Robinson, in correspondence.

62. Kramer, workshop discussion.

63. The Clinton administration took this step in 1995.

64. Since a final agreement is not likely to occur soon, an alternative would be an early declaration of principles that would guide the final agreement. This would likely include the articulation of a final goal of the peace process: two states.

65. Robinson, in correspondence.

66. Yossi Melman, "The Three Faces of Hamas," *Washington Post,* March 10, 1996. A third faction includes "the 'conservative' faction, supported mainly by merchants and traders, [which] advocates a concentration on religious and social issues along with an avoidance of politics and military actions."

67. Barton Gellman, "Hamas May Cooperate with Arafat," *Washington Post,* October 17, 1995.

68. The election results reflect the deep divisions within the Israeli electorate over how best to deal with the Palestinians and the peace process. In the May elections, Benjamin Netanyahu received 1,501,033 votes, or 50.4 percent, while Shimon Peres received 1,471,566 votes, or 49.5 percent. The 120 seats in the 14th Knesset were divided as follows: Labor 34; Likud 32; Shas 10; National Religious Party 9; Meretz 9; Yisrael B'Aliyah 7; Hadash 5; Third Way 4; Yahdut HaTorah 4; United Arab List 4; Moledet 2.

69. *MidEast Mirror* interview with Knesset member Azmi Beshara, May 30, 1996.

70. Douglas Jehl, "For Palestinians, New Sense of Order," *New York Times,* January 16, 1997.

71. Barton Gellman, "Three Palestinians Killed in Hebron," *Washington Post,* April 9, 1997.

4. PAKISTAN AND SOUTH ASIA

1. Mumtaz Ahmad, "Islamic Fundamentalism in South Asia: The Jama'at-i-Islami and the Tablighi Jama'at of South Asia," in *Fundamentalisms Observed,* ed. Martin E. Marty and R. Scott Appleby (Chicago: University of Chicago Press, 1991), 500.

2. Vali Nasr, University of San Diego, "Political Islam in South Asia" (paper presented at the United States Institute of Peace, Washington, D.C., February 3, 1994).

3. Ibid., 1.

4. Kamran Khan, "Fundamentalist Coup Plot Reported in Pakistan," *Washington Post,* October 16, 1995.

5. Nasr, "Political Islam in South Asia," 2.

6. Ahmad, "Islamic Fundamentalism in South Asia," 461.

7. It is argued, however, that while Mawdudi emphasized the need to adapt Islamic principles to modern realities, the earlier reformers sought to "purify Islam of [all] cultural accretions or un-Islamic beliefs." John Esposito, *The Islamic Threat: Myth or Reality?* (New York: Oxford University Press, 1992), 121.

8. Ahmad, "Islamic Fundamentalism in South Asia," 461.

9. "God is the real law-giver and the authority of absolute legislation vest in Him. The believers cannot resort to totally independent legislation nor can they modify any law which God has laid down, even if the desire to effect such legislation or change in Divine laws is unanimous." Abu-l-Ala Mawdudi, "Political Theory of Islam," in *Islam in Transition,* ed. John J. Donohue and John L. Esposito (New York: Oxford University Press, 1982), 253.

10. Esposito, *Islamic Threat,* 122.

11. Mawdudi, "Political Theory of Islam," 256.

12. Ahmad, "Islamic Fundamentalism in South Asia," 466.

13. Ibid., 462.

14. Ibid., 469.

15. Charles Adams, "Mawdudi and the Islamic State," in *Voices of Resurgent Islam,* ed. John L. Esposito (New York: Oxford University Press, 1983), 111.

16. Ahmad, "Islamic Fundamentalism in South Asia," 474.

17. Ibid., 476.

18. Neither the Objectives Resolution of 1949 nor the 1956 constitution went so far as to make Islam the state religion. That such provisions were adopted under a socialist regime is understandable only in light of the powerful resonance of Islam among the electorate, and the inherent strength of Islam as a legitimating force in Pakistani politics, irrespective of party affiliation.

19. Nasr, "Political Islam in South Asia," 7. Bhutto's policies between 1971 and 1977 had created widespread dissent that the Jama'at was able to use to its advantage.

20. See Nasr, "Political Islam in South Asia," 5.

21. Adams, "Mawdudi and the Islamic State," 109.

22. Nasr, "Political Islam in South Asia," 8.

23. "Islam is the glue that keeps the disparate ethnic communities together." Nasr, "Political Islam in South Asia," 7.

24. "Faced with the almost insuperable problems of organizing a state, of dealing with refugees, and of conducting the war in Kashmir, the politicians appealed to Muslim religious sentiments as a means of rallying, unifying, and pacifying the population. It was made to seem that Islam contained the resolution of all difficulties, the one possibility for a true paradise on earth. The result was a wave of enthusiasm for an Islamic polity that swept over Pakistan, leaving the authorities little choice but to accede." Adams, "Mawdudi and the Islamic State," 107.

25. Ahmad, "Islamic Fundamentalism in South Asia," 500.

26. Robert Oakley, National Defense University, workshop discussion.

27. Ahmad, "Islamic Fundamentalism in South Asia," 486.

28. Nasr, workshop discussion.

29. Ahmad, "Islamic Fundamentalism in South Asia," 509.

30. Nasr, workshop discussion.

31. Paula Newberg, Carnegie Endowment for International Peace, workshop discussion.

32. Sugata Bose, Tufts University, workshop discussion.

33. Nasr, "Political Islam in South Asia," 13.

34. Ahmad, "Islamic Fundamentalism in South Asia," 504.

35. Bose, workshop discussion.

36. While its sister organizations see secularism and religion as antagonistic, the Jama'at of India makes a distinction between secularism as an ideology and secularism as a "state policy which implies that there should be no discrimination or partiality on the basis of religious belief." Ahmad, "Islamic Fundamentalism in South Asia," 504.

37. Nasr, "Political Islam in South Asia," 12.

38. Ibid., 13.

39. Oakley, workshop discussion.

40. Many Kashmiris reject both Indian and Pakistani claims to the region.

41. Bose, workshop discussion.

42. Nasr, workshop discussion.

43. John Ward Anderson and Kamran Khan, "Pakistan Shelters Islamic Radicals," *Washington Post,* March 8, 1995.

44. Nasr, "Political Islam in South Asia," 24. Pakistan's foreign secretary, Najamuddin A. Sheikh, is reported as saying that "the underlying problem is religious extremism, fueled by sectarian clashes between Pakistan's majority Sunni and minority Shi'ite Muslims." Anderson and Khan, "Pakistan Shelters Islamic Radicals."

45. Nasr, "Political Islam in South Asia," 20.

46. Ibid., 25.

47. Ibid., 26.

48. "Kashmir is awash in U.S. arms" that have come via the Afghan network. Rena Fonseca, United States Institute of Peace, workshop discussion. It should be noted that arms from the Soviet Union and China also ended up in Kashmir via India.

49. Anderson and Khan, "Pakistan Shelters Islamic Radicals."

50. "Extremism on the subcontinent is not unknown, but activist extremism and access to weaponry is new." Bharat Karnad, Stimson Center, workshop discussion.

51. Oakley, workshop discussion.

52. Ibid.

53. Nasr, workshop discussion.

54. "'Pakistan on its own cannot just go and shut down' terrorist training camps, religious schools, and other places used as terrorist fronts." John Burns, "Pakistan Asks for U.S. Help in Crackdown on Militants," *New York Times,* March 22, 1995.

55. Kenneth J. Cooper, "Indian-Pakistani Cold War Shifts to Nuclear Match Up," *Washington Post,* 5 April 1996.

56. Newberg, workshop discussion.

57. Oakley, in correspondence.

58. Paula Newberg, testimony before the Subcommittee on Asia and the Pacific, Committee on Foreign Affairs, U.S. House of Representatives.

6. INDONESIA

1. The remaining 10 percent are Christian, Hindu, Buddhist, Confucian, and animist. Indonesian Muslims are almost all Sunni.

2. William Liddle of Ohio State University opened the discussion with a paper presentation, followed by a response from Don Emmerson of the University of Wisconsin.

3. Fred R. von der Mehden, "Indonesia," in *The Oxford Encyclopedia of the Modern Islamic World,* ed. John Esposito (New York: Oxford University Press, 1995), 196.

4. East Timor was then under Portuguese rule.

5. Robert Cribb, "Indonesia: History," in *The Far East and Australasia, 1995: Regional Surveys of the World* (London: Europa Publication, 1995), 358.

6. Liddle, workshop discussion.

7. Von der Mehden, "Indonesia," 199.

8. William Liddle, "The Islamic Turn in Indonesia: A Political Explanation" (paper presented at the United States Institute of Peace, Washington, D.C., February 2, 1996), 14.

9. Liddle, "Islamic Turn in Indonesia," 13.

10. Ibid.

11. Ibid., 3.

12. Ibid., 15.

13. The santri are those who "believe and act as pious Muslims (that is, nonsyncretic)," while the abangan are those whose interpretation of Islam does not preclude Hindu, animist, or other influences. In the 1950s and 1960s, the abangan were thought to dominate among Javanese Muslims by almost two to one.

14. More directly in the 1950s when political parties were free to operate, and to a lesser degree today.

15. The Masjumi was the largest Islamic party in the 1950s (although the second largest political party), gaining 21 percent of the vote in the 1955 elections. It was banned in 1959 because of the participation of certain prominent members in the regional rebellions, and because of its continued support for an Islamic state.

16. Because of the army's suspicion of Muslim activists, devout Muslims have historically been discriminated against within the army structure.

17. Liddle, "Islamic Turn in Indonesia," 24.

18. Suharto's pilgrimage to Mecca in 1991 and his subsequent adoption of the name Muhammad would indicate such a shift.

19. Liddle, "Islamic Turn in Indonesia," 3.

20. Ibid., 30.

21. There is a definite tension between the goals of the two dominant groups within ICMI. In terms of economic policy, the technocratic elite seek to promote existing policies of economic development; the Islamic activists, however, "want to use ICMI and the state as a weapon against big private capitalism on behalf of the poor. If they are looking for jobs, it is as state regulators and enforcers of a more egalitarian, less capitalist route to development." Liddle, "Islamic Turn in Indonesia," 11.

22. Ibid., 10.

23. Liddle, workshop discussion. This is particularly true in East Timor, where the majority of the population is of Catholic descent and where politically motivated riots have been seen by some as a pogrom against the minority Muslim community. This, in turn, has generated popular support among Muslims in Java, Sumatra, and elsewhere for cracking down on the East Timorese.

24. Liddle, "Islamic Turn in Indonesia," 8.

25. Emmerson, workshop discussion.

26. Ibid.

27. Identity is a much more fluid phenomenon than many believe. Sidney Jones, Human Rights Watch/Asia, noted that there are no fixed definitions and that a person who may have had a certain religious practice can change when uprooted and moved to a different region.

28. The religious curriculum taught in Indonesian schools tends to be a blend of modernist and traditional thought.

29. Liddle, "Islamic Turn in Indonesia," 19.

30. Emmerson, workshop discussion.

31. This is one of the four central schools of Islamic jurisprudence.

32. On the contrary, according to Madjid, "many forms of government, including that based on *Pancasila,* are in accordance with God's will." Liddle, "Islamic Turn in Indonesia," 19.

33. "Nurcholish himself participated in ICMI's formation, but has maintained a certain distance for the past several years." Liddle, "Islamic Turn in Indonesia," 19–20.

34. Liddle, workshop discussion.

35. Former Jordanian ambassador, Adnan Abu-Odeh, United States Institute of Peace, workshop discussion. Dan Brumberg of Georgetown University noted that the strength of modernist thought is not replicated in the Middle East and North Africa.

36. Former Egyptian ambassador, Tahseen Basheer, United States Institute of Peace, workshop discussion.

37. Liddle, workshop discussion.

38. Basheer, workshop discussion.

39. These include a number of violations, such as torture, disappearance of persons, and the absence of civil liberties (freedom of speech, press, and assembly).

40. Dana Dillon, Department of Defense, workshop discussion.

41. Keith B. Richburg, "Indonesian Panel Faces Toughest Test," *Washington Post,* October 6, 1996.

42. Seth Mydans, "Indonesia Moves Quickly to Suppress a Budding Opposition," *New York Times,* August 7, 1996.

43. The concern with democratic development was used to highlight the absence of political institutions capable of dealing with intercommunal conflict. The absence of such institutions will be particularly relevant when Suharto passes away. Although economic development can mitigate many of the social ills that plague Indonesia, it is not a cure-all, particularly since economic development in that country remains uneven.

44. Emmerson, workshop discussion.

CONCLUSION

1. Glenn Robinson, "To Free the Soul or Free the Nation? The Islamicist Movement in the West Bank and Gaza Strip" (background paper to workshop at the United States Institute of Peace, December 14, 1994), 16.

2. "The government [of Benazir Bhutto] seems to be hamstrung by the fact that it has let the Jama'at be its vehicle for understanding religion in the polity as a whole, rather than looking at what is going on at the grassroots level." Paula Newberg, Carnegie Endowment for International Peace, workshop discussion.

3. In this respect, economic well-being is perceived to be a necessary, though certainly not a sufficient condition for greater cultural openness.

4. For a thorough discussion of Islam and democracy, see Timothy D. Sisk, *Islam and Democracy: Religion, Politics, and Power in the Middle East* (Washington, D.C.; United States Institute of Peace Press, 1992).

5. This is due in large measure to the diversity and tension among Islamic activists, the resiliency of existing governments, and the increasing use of Islam by ruling regimes to support their policies. See Olivier Roy, *The Failure of Political Islam* (Cambridge, Mass.: Harvard University Press, 1994); and Daniel Pearl and Amy Dockser Marcus, "Fundamental Flaw: Political Islam's Hope of Unified Movement Has Failed to Solidify," *Wall Street Journal,* July 5, 1996.

6. Muhammad Faour, *The Arab World after Desert Storm* (Washington, D.C.: United States Institute of Peace Press, 1993), 55.

7. Tahseen Basheer, United States Institute of Peace, speaking at the United States Institute of Peace, Washington, D.C., February 2, 1996.

PARTICIPANTS

The following individuals participated in the conference series "Islamic Activism and U.S. Foreign Policy" held at the United States Institute of Peace between June 1994 and February 1996. The organizations, agencies, and universities listed below reflect the participants' affiliations at the time of the meetings.

MORTON ABRAMOWITZ
Carnegie Endowment for
International Peace

ADNAN ABU-ODEH
United States Institute of
Peace

MARTIN ADAMS
U.S. Department of State

MIKE AMITAY
Helsinki Commission

WALTER ANDERSON
U.S. Department of State

ABDULLAHI AN-NA'IM
Human Rights
Watch/Africa

DOMINIC ASQUITH
Embassy of the United
Kingdom

TOZUN BAHCELI
United States Institute of
Peace

SHAUL BAKHASH
United States Insitute of
Peace

GRAEME BANNERMAN
Bannerman and
Associates

HENRI BARKEY
Lehigh University

TAHSEEN BASHEER
United States Institute of
Peace

DANA BAUER
Central Intelligence
Agency

GEORGE BENSON
United States-Indonesia
Society

JUDITH BIRD
U.S. Department of State

GHASSAN BISHARA
freelance journalist

STEVE BLAKE
U.S. Department of State

SUGATA BOSE
Tufts University

ALASDAIR BOWIE
George Washington
University

DANIEL BRUMBERG
Georgetown University

STEVE BUCK
U.S. Department of State

PATRICIA CARLEY
United States Institute of
Peace

PAULA CAUSEY
U.S. Department of State

JAMES CLAD
Georgetown University

SHAUL COHEN
George Washington
University

LEE COLDREN
U.S. Department of State

THEODORE COLOUMBIS
United States Institute of Peace

JOYCE DAVIS
National Public Radio

DANA DILLON
U.S. Department of Defense

MICHELLE DUNN
U.S. Department of State

DON EMMERSON
University of Wisconsin

JOHN ESPOSITO
Georgetown University

RENA FONSECA
United States Institute of Peace

GRAHAM FULLER
RAND Corporation

SHLOMO GAZIT
United States Institute of Peace

MASOOD GHAZNAVI
Rosemont College

RICKY GOLDSTEIN
Human Rights Watch

YVONNE HADDAD
Amherst College

MORTON HALPERIN
National Security Council

EDWIN HALL
U.S. Senate Committee on Foreign Relations

AHMED HASHIM
Center for Strategic and International Studies

HARRIET HENTGES
United States Institute of Peace

PAUL HENZE
RAND Corporation

SCOTT HIBBARD
United States Institute of Peace

MICHAEL JENDRZEJCZYK
Human Rights Watch/Asia

KENNETH JENSEN
United States Institute of Peace

SIDNEY JONES
Human Rights Watch/Asia

BHARAT KARNAD
Henry L. Stimson Center

STEVE KASHKETT
U.S. Department of State

ZALMAY KHALILZAD
RAND Corporation

BRADY KIESLING
U.S. Department of State

JUDITH KIPPER
Brookings Institution

WILLIAM KIRBY
Search for Common Ground

MARTIN KRAMER
Georgetown University

PAUL KRIESBERG
Woodrow Wilson International Center for Scholars

ELLEN LAIPSON
National Security Council

IAN LESSER
U.S. Department of State

BERNARD LEWIS
Princeton University

SAMUEL LEWIS
U.S. Department of State (retired)

WILLIAM LIDDLE
Ohio State University

DAVID LITT
U.S. Department of State

DAVID LITTLE
United States Institute of Peace

RICHARD LE BARON
U.S. Department of State

RONALD LORTON
U.S. Department of State

HEATH LOWRY
Princeton University

ALAN MAKOVSKY
Washington Institute for Near East Policy

ROBERT MALLEY
National Security Council

SERIF MARDIN
American University

PETE MARTINEZ
U.S. Department of State

EDWARD MASTERS
United States-Indonesia Society

JUDITH MILLER
The New York Times

YEHUDA MIRSKY
U.S. Department of State

RAJA MOHAN
The Hindu

VALI NASR
University of San Diego

PAULA NEWBERG
Carnegie Endowment for
International Peace

MAQSUDUL NURI
Henry L. Stimson Center

SULAYMAN NYANG
Howard University

ROBERT OAKLEY
National Defense
University

MARVIN OTT
National Defense
University

MIKE OWENS
U.S. Department of State

AMIT PANDYA
U.S. House Committee on
Foreign Affairs

CHRIS PANICO
Human Rights
Watch/Helsinki

ROBERT PELLETREAU
U.S. Department of State

CHRISTOPHER PHILLIPS
United States Institute of
Peace

STEVE PIECZENIK
United States Institute of
Peace

WILLIAM QUANDT
University of Virginia

HAROLD RHODE
U.S. Department of
Defense

STEVE RISKIN
United States Institute of
Peace

GOWHER RIZVI
Asia Society

GLENN ROBINSON
Naval Post-Graduate
School

PETER RODMAN
Center for Strategic and
International Studies

ALAN ROMBERG
United States Institute of
Peace

GIDEON ROSE
National Security Council

ABDULAZIZ SACHEDINA
University of Virginia

MOSTAFA-ELWI SAIF
United States Institute of
Peace

ROBERT SATLOFF
Washington Institute for
Near East Policy

ABDUL SATTAR
United States Institute of
Peace

DAVID SATTERFIELD
National Security Council

SABRI SAYARI
Institute of Turkish Studies

RICHARD SCHIFTER
National Security Council

AMIT SEVAK
Henry L. Stimson Center

TIMOTHY SISK
United States Institute of
Peace

JED SNYDER
National Defense
University

SCOTT SNYDER
United States Institute of
Peace

RICHARD SOLOMON
United States Institute of
Peace

ROBERT SPRINGBORG
Chemonics International

GEORGE TANHAM
RAND Corporation

CHRISTINE VICK
Powell, Goldstein, Frazer
& Murphy

CHRIS WEBSTER
U.S. Department of State

ANDREW WHITLEY
Clark and Weinstock

ROBIN WRIGHT
The Los Angeles Times

DAVID WURMSER
Washington Institute for
Near East Policy

MONA YACOUBIAN
U.S. Department of State

I. WILLIAM ZARTMAN
Johns Hopkins University

CHARLES ZENZIE
United States-Indonesia
Society